Powerful Decisions in the Classrooms of Life

Sharon Baker

ISBN:
ISBN-9798579253460

Powerful Decisions in the Classroom of Life Table of Contents

DEDICATION

This book is dedicated to all the students in the classroom of life who are trying to graduate from one level to the next and are tired of being stuck in the same lesson. Here's to you passing your life tests and graduating to the next levels. The growing never ends until you have completed your life assignment.

About the Author

Sharon Baker is a licensed Attorney in Georgia. She also has her Life Insurance and Property & Casualty Insurance licenses.

Some of the different positions she has held throughout her career include:

- Attorney and Partner in a law firm where she specialized in divorce and family law;
- Special Assistant Attorney General where she was assigned to represent the Office of Child Support Enforcement in a judicial circuit in Georgia;
- Part-time Assistant Magistrate Court Judge;
- Assistant District Attorney where she was assigned to represent the Office of Child Support Enforcement in a different judicial circuit in Georgia;
- Unemployment Insurance Tax Chief at the Georgia Department of Labor;
- Financial Services Agent and Life Insurance Agent;
- Director of Disability Adjudication Services at the Georgia Department of Labor and the Georgia Vocational Rehabilitation Agency;
- Contract Attorney;
- Business Owner;
- Probate Court Administrator; and
- Special Projects Manager for a county government in Georgia.

This varied career has prepared Sharon with information and experiences in many different areas. Experience is a great teacher – both through book knowledge and applied first-hand experience. Sharon's passion is that she loves to teach others information that can help them avoid legal pitfalls in life. She even teaches about lessons learned from her own personal mistakes. These lessons can help others to grow faster toward the direction they have set for themselves.

You can contact the author at Sharon@Powerof1Decision.com.

If you have any questions, concerns, or issues or find any errors, please email them to the author. If your corrections are used in future updates of the book, you will be named a "guest editor."

ACKNOWLEDGMENTS

I would like to take this opportunity to thank two groups who made this project possible.

Group One - the individuals who agreed to be interviewed and shared their life lessons with the students reading the lessons. They are:

Ms. Agnes C.
Ms. Angela Christian
Ms. Arleathia Chambliss Wright
Ms. Caroline Harvey Baker
Ms. Carolyn Dickerson
Ms. Delores Dee Lee
Ms. Denise Troutman Holden
Mr. Earnest Francis, Jr.
Retired Col. George Fields
Mr. George Ronald Washington
Mr. JL Harvey
Ms. Karen Baker
Ms. L.S.
Ms. Marchelle Glover
Ms. Marilyn Kenoly

Dr. Mary Christine Cagle
Mr. Melton Tolbert
Mr. Reco McDaniel McCambry
Rev. Claude Ray James
Mr. Rick Dunn
Ms. Shari Moreira
Ms. Smithie Thomas Vaughn
Ms. Sonja Pemberton
Ms. Theresa Barnabei
Mr. Tony Howell
Mr. T. Cole
Ms. Veronica Burge

Group Two – the individuals who financially supported this project before it was published. They are:

Ms. Angela Christian
Ms. Anita Campbell
Ms. Ann Williams
Ms. Aurelia C. Scott
Ms. Bonita Thomas Navarro
Ms. Brenda Gordon
Ms. Carolyn Baker
Ms. Carolyn Dickerson
Mr. Cedric Williams
Ms. Chiquita Adams
Mr. Chuck Baker
Mr. Clarence Marshall
Ms. Clarice Moore
Mr. Daniel Green
Mr. Dewey Perry
Ms. Doris Yates
Ms. Eloise Norris
Ms. Erika McKay
Ms. Frances Wells Smith
Retired Col. George Fields

Mr. Howard Burkat
Mr. JL Harvey
Ms. Karen Baker
Ms. La Fini Gilmer Mosby
Ms. LaToya Long
Ms. LaVerne Brown
Ms. Marchelle Gay
Mr. Martie McLean
Mr. Michael Baker
Mr. Raymond Boykin
Ms. Reba Williams
Ms. Robbie L. Fleming
Ms. Shalada Davis
Ms. Shelia Neely-Norman
Ms. Sonja Pemberton
Ms. Sunya Musawwir
Ms. Sylve Joseph
Ms. Theresa Barnabei
Ms. Toni Whitaker
Ms. Tonya Harris
Ms. Vicki A. R. Smith
Ms. Yolanda DuBose

This is the first book in a series. If you are interested in being interviewed for any subsequent series, please email the author at Sharon@Powerof1Decision.com and use in the subject line – "Interviewed for Your Book" and you will be contacted with information to set up your inclusion.

Again, thank you to the individuals listed in both groups for your support and contributions to the success of this book.

Books by Sharon Baker
Order at Amazon.com or
Contact the author at Sharon@Powerof1Decision.com

	We Can Do THAT?!!! Denzel and Sharon Create Their Perfect Life by Sharon Baker Paperback $19.99 Kindle $0.00 Free with Kindle Unlimited membership Or $4.99 to buy **This is Book 1 of 3 in the *"Denzel and Sharon"* series. In Book 1, they create their perfect life.**
	We Can Do THAT?!!! Denzel and Sharon Create Their Perfect Life: WORKBOOK – YOU Can Do THAT Too?!!!! by Sharon Baker Paperback $8.99 **Workbook for you to Create Your Perfect Life as you follow along with *"Denzel and Sharon."***

Book 2: They Can Do That?!!! Denzel and Sharon Protect Their Perfect Life ("That Book" Series)
by Sharon Baker
Paperback
$19.99

Book 2 of the "*Denzel and Sharon*" - That Book Series. Learn how their children, parents, and siblings can attempt to interfere with *Denzel and Sharon's* Perfect Life. But they were able to Protect the life that they created.

Book 2 Workbook: THEY Can Do THAT?!!! Denzel and Sharon Protect Their Perfect Life (Workbook for You to Protect Your Perfect Life)
by Sharon Baker
Paperback
$8.99

Here is your workbook on how you can follow along with *Denzel and Sharon's* story and address issues from others that may attempt to interfere with "Your Perfect Life."

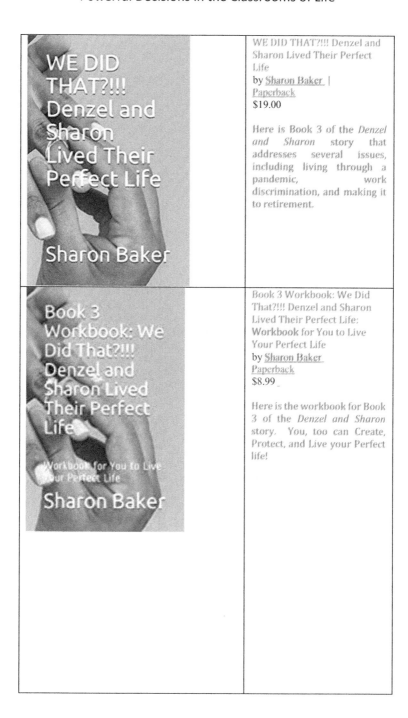

WE DID THAT?!!! Denzel and Sharon Lived Their Perfect Life	WE DID THAT?!!! Denzel and Sharon Lived Their Perfect Life by Sharon Baker | Paperback $19.00 Here is Book 3 of the *Denzel and Sharon* story that addresses several issues, including living through a pandemic, work discrimination, and making it to retirement.
Book 3 Workbook: We Did That?!!! Denzel and Sharon Lived Their Perfect Life	Book 3 Workbook: We Did That?!!! Denzel and Sharon Lived Their Perfect Life: Workbook for You to Live Your Perfect Life by Sharon Baker Paperback $8.99 Here is the workbook for Book 3 of the *Denzel and Sharon* story. You, too can Create, Protect, and Live your Perfect life!

	There is Power in Making a Decision: **Create 2020 Clarity for Your Life** by Sharon Baker Paperback $19.99 Are you Clear on what kind of life you want to create for yourself? Get Clear with this Clarity Workbook.
	POWER OF 1 DECISION CLARITY JOURNAL: **My 90-Day Success Journal** by Sharon Baker Paperback $19.99 *Here is your 90 Day Success Journal to track and hold yourself accountable to achieve all of your goals and dreams for your successful life.*

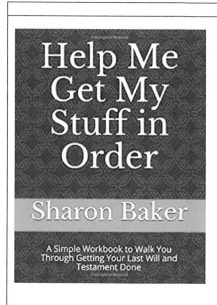	Help Me Get My Stuff in Order: A Simple Workbook to Walk You Through Getting Your Last Will and Testament Done by Sharon Baker Paperback $19.99 This Workbook walks you through the process of reviewing your stuff and deciding who you want to have your stuff when you die. Do you know what happens when you die with or without a Will? Do you know where to get legal help?
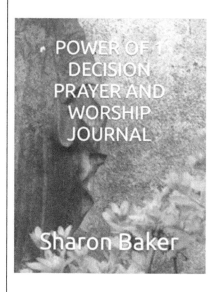	**POWER OF 1 DECISION PRAYER AND WORSHIP JOURNAL** by Sharon Baker Paperback $19.99 **Power of 1 Decision Prayer and Worship Journal is designed to help you to record your daily prayers, bible app notes, daily devotion notes, church sermons, and Church/Sunday School notes all in one place to help you grow to the next level in your spiritual life.**

HOMEROOM CLASS

Teacher: Welcome to the Classrooms of Life. This is your Homeroom, and I am your Homeroom Teacher, Ms. Baker. We will be examining the process of making powerful decisions in the classrooms of life:

- Spiritual Classroom;

- Family and Relationships Classroom;

- Education and Career Classroom;

- Health and Wellness Classroom;

- Financial Classroom; and

- Estate Planning Classroom.

Before we go to these classrooms, let's discuss some of the basics. What are **Decisions**? We've all made them, and we make them every day. Some are instinctive, some are habitual, some are made unconsciously, and some are powerful. A decision is defined as the act or process of deciding something or of resolving a question, making a formal judgment, the act or need for making up one's mind, and winning victory over. Making a decision can also be the process resulting in the selection of a course of action among several alternative scenarios. Every decision-making process produces a final choice. We usually weigh the pros and cons before making a final decision that fits our needs.

Decisions can be based on many different influences:

A) Some decisions can be psychologically based – influenced by the needs and values of the individual.

B) Some decisions can be normatively based – using logic and rational thinking that ends when a satisfactory solution is reached. Logic on the other hand is the application of knowledge in making informed decisions.

C) Some decisions are based on emotions – the feelings and desires of the individual.

Which type is yours?

We need to be clear that making a decision of any type is not the same as conducting an analysis. An analysis is the study of an issue; however, no action is taken and no solution is reached. Sometimes, one can suffer from analysis paralysis. A situation where one over-analyzes and overthinks so that no decision or action is ever taken, and the result is paralyzing themselves over the outcome.

Let's get back to decisions. There are four benefits of the decision-making process: establishing goals, measurement of progress, action taken, and application of resources in an orderly way. There are also steps in making decisions. According to Dr. Pam Brown, there are seven steps in making a decision. They are:

1. Outline your goal and outcome,

2. Gather data,

3. Develop alternatives,

4. Weigh the pros and cons of each alternative,

5. **Make a decision** (emphasis added),

6. Immediately take action to implement it, and

7. Learn from and reflect on the decision.

However, even in the most perfect system and steps followed, some biases can and do creep into the decision-making process. These biases include the following: selective search for evidence, premature termination of evidence, wishful thinking, cultural perceptions, recent information, repetition of information until believing it is true, peer pressure, and prejudices. There may also be other things that one may not even be aware of that can have an impact on the decision-making process.

After going through all of that, what makes a decision **Powerful**? Power is defined as the energy, ability, capacity to do something, control, authority, influence over another, and the ability to act or produce an effect. Now, that's power.

Being at an intersection of life, sometimes, life forces you to make a decision, mostly out of desperation and necessity instead of purposefully. Your spiritual being has an impact on your decisions. God has a way of shifting events in your life to move you towards a pre-determined destination. God's process is not always fun and enjoyable, especially going through the valley of the shadow of death. You have to keep moving though.

In life, we are sometimes teachers and sometimes students and sometimes we are both. As teachers in the classrooms of life, we can share our lessons learned so that they are blueprints of success for other students sitting in those classrooms to follow. As students in the classrooms of life, we can learn some valuable information, knowledge, and lessons from our own experiences or from the lessons of others who have gone before us. These lessons have helped us to make powerful decisions in order to take powerful actions that lead us to achieve the desired powerful goals and results. Students learn those lessons through various methods – first-hand experience, reading, modeling others' actions and behaviors, and imitating others.

As stated before, the life classrooms we will examine consist of spiritual classes, relationship classes, financial classes, educational/career classes, family classes, health classes, and fun classes. Each class will explore the process of making powerful decisions. Also in each of these classes, real-life individuals are going to teach and share that one powerful decision that they made. Each person has been willing to share what they have learned with the class.

Also In each classroom, just like in life, there is an exam. If you fail the exam, you find yourself having to re-take the exam over and over and over until you pass or you will forever be in that classroom grade. You don't get promoted to the next level. This promotion has nothing to do with age, sex, race, nationality, origin, background, finances, or anything else. Everyone must take and pass their own exams. In each of the defined classrooms, you find yourself at a different level and grade. Some classmates are in pre-school, elementary, middle, high school, college, trade school, graduate school, or post-graduate school in each life classroom. But know that there is no final classroom exam until death. If you are still breathing, you are still in each classroom learning as a student or teaching a lesson to others or both.

Before we start moving into the different classrooms, here is the **first homework**. We are going to look at the different classrooms of life, and you are to answer the overarching questions:

1. What Do You Want; and

2. Why Do You Want It?

Here is an example: "In the classroom of health, you may want to lose weight from your current weight of _____ to your goal weight of _____. Why you want it is because you want to be healthy and live a long and fruitful life."

If you are going to learn about these classrooms of life, you and only you can decide what kind of life you want and why you want it. Let's examine some additional terms that we must be clear about. **Goals are what** we want and our **Purpose is why** we want them. Goals are the results of achievement toward which effort is directed; what I am aiming at; the end result. Purpose is an intended or desired result; the reason for which something exists or is done, made, or used.

So class, did you do your first homework? If so, congratulations! Now, it's time to go to the classrooms.

CHAPTER 1: POWERFUL DECISIONS IN THE CLASSROOM OF YOUR SPIRITUAL LIFE

Teacher: Good morning class. Here is how each classroom will operate. First, I will give some introductory comments on the classroom. Second, we will have an interview with the guest who is going to share with us their powerful decision. Last, we will have homework to do. Let's get ready class for some exciting information.

Today, we are going to talk about your spiritual life. We have 4 special guests who are going to talk about the Powerful

Decisions that they have made in this classroom. Here are some initial questions for your class to answer:

- Do you believe in God?

- Do you believe in Jesus?

- Do you believe in the Holy Spirit?

- Are you a religious person?

- Are you a spiritual person?

- Do you attend a place of worship?

- Have you been baptized?

- Do you read the Bible?

Did you answer all of these questions? Let's discuss our spiritual life.

Have you wondered where you came from? Take time right now and focus on your breathing, what you see around you, what you hear around you, what you are feeling around you, and what you are smelling around you. There is a whole universe and we are only a small part of it. Look at the sky, the trees, and the ocean and realize that there must be something in control of all of this. Man did not create it and man cannot control it. If he could, then man would figure out a way to use it to his advantage and to the disadvantage of others. Life is filled with mystery that man has yet to grasp or figure out how and where did it all come from.

Class, I am not a minister and do not have any formal biblical training, but I believe in the God of the universe, who created everything, including you and me. Each person must get to a place of understanding his or her connection to the Creator, God. Either you will get to that place of acceptance or you will reject that connection. But I believe everyone will have an encounter where they will be faced with a decision to choose between connecting to and disconnecting from God. You have free will to make a decision. You are not a robot that has been preprogrammed to choose your connection. I believe that everyone's encounter will be different, but will be monumental for that person's growth. Some have their encounters early in their lives and some later, but it will happen. When you look around and acknowledge that there is something bigger than you that is in control of this place called Earth, then you will begin the journey toward making a connection with God.

Teacher: So class, our first guest speaker is Pastor Claude Ray James. Pastor James, can you tell us a little about yourself?

Pastor James: I live in Georgia. I have a master's degree in Christian Education from the ITC – Interdenominational Theological Center and I have a B.A. from Glassboro State College in Glassboro, NJ. I retired in May 2019. I have pastored several African Methodist Episcopal churches in Georgia. Prior to going into ministry, I served in the United States Air Force and after I got out, I was a police officer in Camden, NJ, and worked at the Federal Bureau of Prisons in Tallahassee, FL.

Teacher: Pastor James, talking about God and Spirituality can be a very intense subject. I know that it requires a lot. You are a retired pastor in the A.M.E. Church. Can you talk to us briefly about making the powerful decision about our individual relationship, knowledge, and understanding of God and Spirituality?

Pastor James: The original creation of God was a spirit creation. God is the spirit. When you read the Bible and you do some research, you discover that in the Book of Isaiah 14, and the Book of Ezekiel 28, there was another character in there. Because this is so broken in pieces let me try to put it in some order. In the creation of God, of His universe, not just earth, because you hear about God creating the heavens and the earth. But He created everything and there are other planets out there.

After earth is where God, after the creation, put His government over the earth. He delegated authority to Lucifer. You will find Lucifer in Isaiah 14, and Ezekiel 28. But at some point in his rulership, he – Lucifer decided that he wanted to be above God. And in that process, the other angelic hosts tried all they could to get that idea out of his head. He kept it in there. So, eventually, there was a Great War in heaven. The war was between the forces of light and the forces of darkness. God is light. Lucifer, the word itself means bringer of light, but he decided that in the process of his rulership that he wanted to be above God. In other words, if you read this whole thing you will find that in his process of trying to dethrone God, there was a war in heaven. The result of the angelic war, you ended up with what you have now – chaos.

If you notice all the planets are destroyed of them. Earth was destroyed too, but our Bible opens up with God re-healing the earth for new creation. So, it says, in the beginning, God created the heavens and the earth. That was complete. It was completed at that point. Then it says, in the Hebrew Bible, that the earth was void. It became void because of the great spiritual battle that took place. Then God began to re-heal it for a new creation. But He did not destroy Lucifer or as God changes his name from Lucifer to Satan. The word Satan means adversary of God. When this was destroyed, God did not destroy him. He redid the earth for new creation, which is physical, which is the man.

So, God created Adam and Eve. If you read in Genesis 1:27-28, this is what He said: "and God created man in His own image, in the image of God created He them - male and female." They were created equal. They had different tasks though. A hog's task and a cow's task are different. They are two different animals. But the same God made them both. They got two different roles to play. So, this same thing happened with Adam and Eve. God said but He blessed them and said to them be fruitful and multiply and replenish the earth. In other words, God is rebuilding His earth through physical man.

You are a child of God. You were born that way. He created you. Your first real parent is Adam. According to the scripture, everybody, says well, we are all children of Adam. What is it that Adam had that we all have? Later on, he sinned. So, he sinned before he had children. He passed that on to all of his descendants.

Now, there are three parts to God, don't forget this. We say God is a Trinity, right? Then some people want to argue that God can't be 3 persons. Well, they don't know math very well. Let me say this to you, let's take the SUN, the sun. There is one sun that we can see. There may be a whole lot more scientists say are out there. But there is one that we do see. It is absolutely the master of the universe. It gives life to everything, is that right? Now, the sun is the trinity. First of all, it gives you heat. You can't see heat. But you can feel the heat. Ok, that represents the Father. You can't see Him, but oh my God you can feel Him. The sun gives you light. The light represents the son, Jesus. Jesus says I am the light of the world. Then the sun gives you energy. That's what hits the earth and gives life to it. So, does that represents the Holy Spirit?

The reason I want to talk about this is that I want you to understand that there are two dominant spirits in the world. There is the spirit of God that the Bible talks about all through it; and there's a spirit of Satan, which is a selfish, rebellious spirit.

And that's the one we were born with. That's who we are. How do I know we're born with it? Do you think a little baby cares that he wakes you up at 3:00 in the morning to come back there to change his diaper and feed him? He does not care that you have to get up at 6:00 a.m. to go to work. It is always about them and what they want. It is selfishness and we are born with it. That's who we are. The reason I'm saying this is because I want you to see I was born with that. But I didn't know that when I was a child, I just wanted to have my way and you did too. You did the same thing. Now if the parents were strong enough, they would try to break that part of you. Not when you were a baby, but when you grew up as long as you understand. I can't go along with that because I will be doing all this for her or him. So, let me make you understand now that you can't have your way. This is the problem right now.

I'm saying that there are 2 dominant spirits in the world - that is the spirit of God, which is good, and there's spirit of Satan, that's selfishness. Now, what is it about Satan, what is one of his characteristics? Jesus said that he's a liar. (See Saint John 8:32-44). Just as God has children, Satan too has children. One of their dominant characteristics is lying. So, these dominant spirits in the world we all have because as children we don't know we have them.

Teacher: Well, that's the difference because when you boil it down either God is running your life or Satan is running your life.

Pastor James: Yes, well, let me say this to get back to the three parts of God. We talked about heat, light, and energy. Is that correct?

Truthfully, all of us have three parts. We have a body, mind, and spirit. But there is one you. Now, this spirit is part of us, until God's spirit comes into you. You still have the old spirit, which is satanic and selfishness. All sin is rooted in that one thing, selfishness. It's what you want for yourself over what God wants for you. When you let your will be dominant, it becomes a sin because we make sin such a terrible thing. That's why when we do communion, we say Lord forgive us for our sins of thoughts, words, and deeds. It is constantly with us all the time. When you are aware it's there, then you can deal with it. But if you're not, you will think you're right. You'll be arguing from now on that you are right. Nobody is admitting that they are wrong.

Teacher: Is this where the brokenness comes from?

Pastor James: Yes, brokenness is always there. All things are broken. Even when we fix it, it gets broken again. It will always be broken until Christ comes again to reestablish God's Kingdom on earth. As I said to you prior that God's kingdom rules the earth. So, when Christ came and told us to pray for the Kingdom because the only thing that will bring peace to our world is God's Kingdom because the kingdoms of man are all corrupt. All you got to do is watch the news every day. Everybody is rising up against the political leaders, not just here but all over the world. Every nation has people who are upset with the government. We are moving to the time when God's Kingdom will come. He promised it. It is the only thing that will solve the world's problems. When we think of a church, we think it will be holy, walking around, and shouting all over the place. That is not what it is. It is the Kingdom of God. It is a Kingdom of righteous people. It is a Kingdom where God will come and change our nature. So said 1 John 3: 1-2 and 1 Corinthians 15, that after the resurrection, Paul talks about what we will be like. I mean we die, we are buried, and we rot in the ground. When Christ comes, He will raise that body again, and put new life in it. In other words, you won't even have blood. You have eternity with you if you are of God.

You follow what I am saying. So, when you read in scripture, what does the scripture say? Just turned to 1 Corinthians 15 and read the whole thing if you want to because it talks about resurrection. But if you really want to know about what kind of bodies we come with, you start reading from 1 Corinthians 15:32 and read down to the end of the chapter. It gives you a good description of what we will be like when Christ comes and change these bodies, these resurrected bodies.

I did say something to you about resurrection, didn't I? The thing that holds us up in this life is the Doctrine of Resurrection. Some don't believe there is such a thing. But I said this to you, God shows us every year that resurrection is a reality. How does He do that? If you look at the plant world. When I was in high school, we had a course called Vocational Agriculture. My project was a garden and every spring I will go out there and prepare the ground for planting. Once you've done that, you got your hose, your fertilizer, and all that stuff. You would take dead seeds; it would be peas or corn or squash or whatever it is. You put those dead seeds into the ground. In seven to nine days, there is something on the earth that would give them life again. Then you see a little green stem shoot up from under the ground. Whatever it is, the seed is dead before you plant it. Therefore, if God will do this for a dead seed what do you think He would do for us who are made in His image? Resurrection is reality. It is reality. It happens. It is going to happen. It happens every year but we just don't pay it any attention. We are not focused. We don't see spiritual things; we just see physical things. We see it and we don't understand it. You could take some peas right and then go down and I don't know whether you have a yard in your backyard or not. But when you did go out there next March and prepare the soil and put those seeds in the ground, I guarantee you they will not stay down there. They will get up, break through the earth, come up, and the next thing you know is you got a bush. Then the next thing you know you got some peas on it. Why? Because resurrection is a reality. If God will do that to some peas and corn and okra, what do you think He will do for those who are born and made in His image? Resurrection is real.

So, when you read about Salvation, you wanna go to Romans 10:9. It says if thou will confess with thy mouth the Lord Jesus Christ, confessing and believe in thy heart that God raised him from the dead, believe, thou shall be saved. Salvation is so simple most people will miss it. They think they gotta go jump over that pew and jump cross that pew. That had nothing to do with it. That's your mess. But it is so simple and that's the spiritual side of life. If you don't know that, you will go to church all of your life and still not know anything. Because if your preacher is not teaching, I feel sorry for the congregation. The good news is that everything you need to know is in the Book, the Bible.

Teacher: How did you make the Powerful Decision to go into ministry? Was it a pulling of you or did someone help steer you in that direction?

Pastor James: No, here's what it was. All of my life from the time I was a little boy. I remember when my mother bought a Bible from the Watkin's liniment man. You would not know anything about that. You may be too young for that one. These people used to go around in their cars selling stuff. I remember when my mother bought a Bible. When my dad got out of World War II, when I was born, he was in Europe. When he came home, I was almost two years old. He built a house and got a job at the railroad. My mother bought that Bible and learned to read the Bible to us. I never had to be made to go to church. I loved to go to church and hear the choir sing. As a matter of fact, I had a terrible problem in school. I used to stutter. I stuttered so much in class that I couldn't even read. I knew the word, but I couldn't get it out. It was my 8th-grade teacher, Miss B.W. She is dead now. I remember one day, she said Claude James, you can read. This problem you got, you gonna get rid of it one day. I had no idea that woman knew what she was talking about. I must have been in the 9th or 10th grade. At service one day, the preacher, Reverend Green, preached about Moses' encounter with God. When God told him that He wanted him to go to Egypt. Moses said to God, I've got a terrible speech problem. Now take my brother Aaron. See now, he can talk. He can articulate this thing. Moses, what is your problem? Lord, now I really stutter too much. Is that right? OK. Then God asked him the question, who made man's mouth Moses, was it not I?

That was the first time I heard that and I could not believe it. Who made your mouth? The kids used to laugh at me when I tried to read. That's what kids do; they laugh when they see something. It doesn't have to be funny but they laugh. I remember my prayers consistently. Lord, I don't want to be better than anybody, but I'm so sick and tired of these kids laughing at me. I cried for many days about them laughing at me. I do not remember when it passed. I don't remember anything but I know that I stutter no more. I said wow. So, I know from personal experience God has dealt with my life. I don't go saying it too much, but I will throw it in there from personal experience that God will change your life if you allow Him to do that. He won't break the door down, but if you let Him do it, He'll do it for you. And people will wonder how it happened.

My cousin, who lives in Woodstock now, used to live in California until 2007 when he moved to Atlanta. I went into the Air Force, it was about the same time when he went into the Army. One day, he went home and asked about me, he was amazed when someone told him that I was preaching. He said that I couldn't because I stuttered in class. He insisted that there is no way that I could speak. So, when he told me what he said,

I said you are absolutely correct; but what you don't know is what I know. That there is a God who made man's mouth? God did it for me. So, you have to give credit to God. In other words, God has put a lot of things in your life spiritually that you may not have recognized at the time. But when you reflect on it, you wonder. Suppose if I have not done that, where would I have been? There are things you recognize that you should have done when you didn't do them. You realize that you should have done that. It wasn't that it didn't come to me, it came to me. It was very clear, but I just thought I gotta stay there. Now, there are some things God listens to when you are in tune with God. A lot of people don't know that prayer is not just articulating prayer. Sometimes, it's just listening to hear from God Himself.

Dr. Jonathan Jackson, who is dead now, was in charge of the Christian Education Department at ITC. He taught most of those classes and those who were in that Department. I remember one day we went to class. He said everybody should close their books, shut their eyes, and put their head on the desk until he told them to hold their head up. He did that for about 5 minutes. He said, now open your eyes and hold your head up. Then he went around the class and said now what did you hear? He started with the first student. He told what he heard - the kids out there playing, they heard the birds, they heard the sirens going by, they heard people walking across the campus. Everybody told what they heard because they were listening. He said, now you need to learn to do this if you gonna do ministry. You have to learn to find a quiet place somewhere in your house. I know you got your wife there, you got your husband there, and the children are there too. If you gotta go to the bathroom and lock the door, listen. God will speak to you. It won't be audible or anything like that because if He spoke to you audibly, you would tear the door down and run out of there. There's a still small voice that will speak to you. You will need some time to yourself. I don't know how you will do it, but you have to make some time for yourself. You will be surprised by what comes to you. Write down these things that come to you. If you don't write it down at the moment, when you think about it later, you will not remember it to save your life. God will speak to you. He will speak to you if you let Him. But you gotta be on guard to listen and be able to put it down. You'd be surprised. Sometimes, these words you get are like tomato seeds. Write it down and put it all in a notebook somewhere. You will get some religious writings that you're not gonna fully understand. Don't throw it away. Put it in a notebook. When you grow to it, you say you know I'm glad I saved this. Wow, I didn't know it meant that. But so often we live in the moment and forget that every day should be a learning experience. So, sometimes, when you are home and you get your Bible, turn to Romans 10:9. In that particular verse, it's a powerful thing for any personal Salvation. *"If you would but confess with your mouth The Lord Jesus Christ and believe in your heart that God raised Him from the dead, you shall be saved."* Now, that has nothing to do with you jumping over the pew or acting crazy. Salvation is so simple that most people will miss it. Unless you have a teacher that'll help you with it, you will miss the whole thing. So, I hope I'm making some sense of what I'm trying to share with you.

Teacher: Thank you Pastor James for sharing with us about the Powerful Spiritual Decision. Is there anything else that you want to share with us?

Pastor James: Let me give you one more thing before I go.   In your Bible, Ezekiel 28:13, is another reading of Lucifer/Satan/the fallen Angel. It reads, *"Thou has been in Eden the garden of God, every precious stone was thy covering, the sardius, topaz, and diamond, beryl, onyx and jasper, the sapphire, turquoise, and the emerald with gold.   The workmanship of your timbrels and pipes was prepared for you on the day you were created.   You were the anointed cherub who covers."* In other words, he was the big shot and I have set thee so. Thou was upon the holy mountain. When you see the word "mountain" in the Old Testament, it is symbolic of government. Thou was upon the holy mountain of God. Thou has walked up and down in the midst of the fire. Thou was perfect in the way from the day that thou was created. God made him perfect till iniquity alone is found in you. By the multitude of the merchandise, they have filled in the midst of thee with violence. Thou has sinned. Therefore, I will cast thee as a profane out of the mountain. I know the government of God and I have assured thee, oh covering cherub. When you read this, you find that this is Satan speaking in heaven. Satan is one of the highest archangels in charge of the whole heaven - a third of the heavenly host on earth. God put him on earth to rule it. This is where he was. One person asked why then did God create him and just get rid of him. Well, answering the above question, Ellen G. White wrote in his book called "The Great Controversy Between Christ and Satan", if God would have destroyed him, the 2/3 of the angels that were a part of the heavenly host would have been worshipping God out of fear. And God doesn't want you to worship Him in fear. God wants you to worship Him because God loves you and He wants you to love Him back. He wants you to do it under an act of love. So, He gave him some time to rule the world until He showed the other 2/3 of the angels what Satan's rule would bring about. It brought about God destroying the earth the first time with water and then it talks about God promising that He would do it again by fire. In other words, He is giving Satan 6000 years to rule, but the earth is much older than that. God is eternal. We are near the time when Christ will come again.   And the Christ, who came the first time, the peaceful gentle giant is coming again soon to undo the working of Satan.

Then let me put it this way: Adam fell to three things, I'm talking about sin now. Listen to what happened. And the woman saw the fruit, that's the lust of the eye. And it was good for food, that's the lust of the flesh. And it was desired to make one wise, that's the pride of life. All sin comes under one of those three categories.   Now, Christ came to undo what Adam had done. So, when Christ walked the earth, immediately after He was baptized, which was a commission to start His work, the Bible said in Matthew and in Luke that He was driven to the wilderness to be tempted by the devil. The same devil who tripped up Adam is gonna try to trip up the second Adam, which is Christ. The difference in this is if you read those two chapters - Matthew 4 & Luke 4, the response that Christ had with Satan is different from what Adam had. So, after 40 days Christ became hungry, and the devil showed up. "If you be..." In other words, he's playing with Christ's ego; if you be God's Son, then why don't you just turn these stones into bread? Well, what he did not know was that Christ had no ego. He knows exactly who He is. And He said man shall not live by bread alone. What is Christ doing? He is quoting scripture. Christ said, it is written, man should not live by bread alone. For everything that Lucifer said, Christ said, it is written. In other words, the book that we live by is the Bible. And keep in mind, the Old Testament was not given to Christians. We can use it because there's a lot of information that makes Christianity worthwhile; but that book was given exclusively to Jews or to Abraham's children, the Hebrew people. Christ came to bring in a new people, of the Gentile nation. When you are dealing with scripture, you need to understand to who the message is given. I'll put it that way. There was no Christian in the Old Testament. Christ was not a Christian. Christ was a Jew. He was born a Jew. He lived as a Jew. He died a Jew. Christianity came about in the book of Acts when they called those Jews who follow Christ Christians. They call them Christian in a city called Antioch because they were Christ-like. Those people followed Christ religiously.

Oh, I'm sorry that I took you all around like that, but it's the spiritual things in life that keep us together. I want to share it with you before I go. Before this interview started, I was having a pity party for myself. I remember the song that I had heard and it's getting me out of the root I was in. Boy, did it pick me up? Wow. I shouldn't be crying and feeling sorry for myself. Man, God has blessed you in every kind of way and you are sitting here having a pity party. Come on. You have no business with a pity party. Don't do that. This song is entitled, "Remind Me Dear Lord" by the Sensational Nightingales. Because there are some things that when we are having these parties for ourselves, God needs to remind us of stuff. That got me out of my mess. Lord, I just need to be reminded. You brought me from where I was sitting and crying. Get up from there, you chastised me. You better get up and go praise the Lord. He didn't have to do all of this stuff He just does. Wow. In other words, we just need to be reminded of what God has already done. I'm telling you it will get you out of your mess sometime, out of your rut, because we all get in ruts. But if you want to hear that song sometime, just pull it up on your phone and tap in there the Sensational Nightingales and the song is entitled "Remind Me Dear Lord."

Teacher: Thank you so much Pastor James for sharing with us about God and Spirituality.   Class, I know that was a lot to unpack; but we thank you Pastor James for helping us with this lesson.

Class, our second speaker to talk to us about his Spiritual Powerful Decision is Mr. George Ronald Washington. Welcome to the Spiritual Classroom and tell us a little about yourself.

Mr. Washington: Thanks for having me and allowing me to talk to the class about my Spiritual Decision. I live in Maryland and I am a Correctional Officer. Early in my life, I remember this incident when I had a physical altercation with an older man.

After that event, I only had one thing on my mind, and that was to kill this person.

Teacher: Oh, wow.

Mr. Washington: I left that situation to go to my friend's house to get his weapon so I could take care of him. But God intervened with a preacher teaching Bible study at my friend's house. When I got there, I sat and listened. I heard for the first time in my life that Jesus loved me.

Teacher: What did you learn from this decision?

Mr. Washington: I learned that I'm special to God and that my life has a purpose. The time to change is now.

Teacher: How old were you when you made this decision?

Mr. Washington: Fifteen years old.

Teacher: Wow, you were only fifteen years old. How did your life change from this decision?

Mr. Washington: This decision helped me come off a death course to a phenomenal life course. God showed me that He was pursuing me and wanted a relationship with me.

Teacher: Who do you want to thank for helping you to make this decision?

Mr. Washington: E. D. Washington, Pastor S. J. Nicholson, Pastor C. Brooks, and Deacon R. Brown. These people I owe my life to, outside of God. If it weren't for them imparting in my life, I don't know where I would be.

Teacher: What areas of your life were impacted by this decision?

Mr. Washington: My childhood hurts and struggles impacted my life. My name impacted me negatively. Also, the present situation that was going on at the time really took my life in a downhill spiral; but Thanks-Be-To God for interceding on my behalf. Now I have an awesome wife, kids, and a family. Also, I reached a milestone in my life celebrating my 50th birthday and becoming a Deacon in my local church.

Teacher: Anything else about this decision that you want to share?

Mr. Washington: The decision to accept Christ changed my world, and also the people in and around my world! I am forever grateful to God for pulling me out of that terrible world of sin."

Teacher: Thank you again Mr. George Ronald Washington for sharing your Powerful Spiritual Decision with us.

Class, the next person to share their Powerful Spiritual Decision with us is Ms. Delores "Dee" Lee. Hello Ms. Lee and welcome to the classroom. Can you tell us a little about yourself?

Ms. Lee: Thank you for giving me this opportunity to share my Powerful Spiritual Decision. I live in Georgia and I am a retired accounting professional.

In 1996, after my yearly physical, Dr. Hurley, my doctor said she heard something in my heart that she had never heard before and would I mind going for an echocardiogram. I laughed and said, of course, I need my heart. Little did I know they would find a birth defect; I had a hole in my heart! I needed to have surgery on my heart. Realizing that I may not come through the surgery, my prayer to God was:

"Lord, there are only two things that can come from the surgery, I will live or die. Lord, if it is your will and my time to die please let me come home to be with you. Knowing my family will grieve and mourn, please comfort them in knowing that I have come to be with you. But Lord, if it is your will for me to live, please show me what I need to serve you. God I know if you keep me alive, it was for a purpose. Lord, please guide my steps down the path you want me to follow."

Teacher: Wow, Ms. Lee. That is an impressive prayer. How old were you when this happened?

Ms. Lee: At the time of the surgery, I was a 42-year-old mother of a son who was living and working at a school in Japan.

Teacher: How did this change your life?

Ms. Lee: My life changed because I had to deal with my mortality. This made me learn to appreciate family, friends, and the small and large things in my life. My greatest helper in making this decision was God Almighty. Once I prayed, He gave me that blessed assurance and I was at peace. I knew in my heart that either choice would be a win-win situation for me. This decision caused me to have a more intimate relationship with the Lord. I felt a presence with God that I had never felt before. God allowed me to be at peace with Him. My life changed from making decisions alone to now asking God for His guidance in my life.

Teacher: Thank you so much Ms. Lee for sharing with us. Class our next speaker in this classroom is Ms. Veronica Burge. Please introduce yourself to the class, Ms. Burge.

Ms. Burge: I live in Tampa, Fl. I have an MBA and currently, work as a Pharmaceutical Commercial Sales Manager.

The Powerful Spiritual Decision I made in my life was to trust God in every aspect of my life. Throughout my life, I was taught to always seek God and live in a way that is pleasing to God. The one thing that I didn't truly incorporate into my life until I entered my 40s was trusting God with everything. To truly trust that and be led by God and trusting that He controls the outcome of my path did not resonate with me earlier in my life. While I am a believer, I focused on worldly things at times in my life as guidance versus seeking God first and trusting Him. While my life is not perfect, I now understand that God has a plan for everything in me and my trust in Him is why I embrace what happens in my life.

Teacher: What did you learn from this Powerful Spiritual Decision?

Ms. Burge: I learned that seeking God first and not my own thinking has far better results in my life.

Teacher: How old were you when you made this decision?

Ms. Burge: I was 41 years old.

Teacher: Wow! How did your life change from this decision?

Ms. Burge: My life changed in many areas. One specific area is my career. I trusted God and prayed for His guidance in my career. I focused on listening to God versus making career decisions with Him. This allowed me to become open to a new environment, a new city, and a company to grow my career.

Teacher: Who do you want to thank for helping you to make this decision?

Ms. Burge: I thank my mother for being supportive and helping me to trust God first.

Teacher: What areas of your life were impacted by this decision?

Ms. Burge: My career, my lifestyle, the people I chose as friends, and how I treated others.

Teacher: Is there anything else about this decision that you want to share?

Ms. Burge: I would like to share that choosing God first is the greatest decision I have made in my life. No matter what happens in my life, I am at peace because I know God is in control.

Teacher: Thank you so much Ms. Burge for sharing.

Classroom Closing and Homework:

Class, as you can see from all of the speakers today, making a Powerful Spiritual Decision can truly change your life for the better. Each person had their own unique encounter with God at different times in their lives and at different ages. Each one of us will also have a personal encounter and the decision that we make from that encounter will shape who we become as individuals.

Let me leave you with this. There are many types of religions that exist in the world. Each has its own set of beliefs, customs, and traditions. Each person has to find their own way to a place where their connection with God is nurtured, fed, and enhanced. At its core, God is LOVE. HE loves each and every one of us so much that HE wants the best for each of us. HE wants us to be with HIM, both now and forever. Man, with his free will, wants a lot of things, some good and some bad. But God will allow the man to make up his own mind.

Most of you have probably heard of the story of Adam and Eve. If you haven't, then I suggest that you read the book of Genesis and the creation of man and woman. God created Adam and his helpmeet, Eve, and they lived in the Garden of Eden. All of their needs were met and God communed with them. One day, Eve met with the devil, and he deceived her by telling her to do what God had told Adam not to do, which was to eat from the tree of good and evil. Eve ate the forbidden fruit and gave some to Adam, who also ate the forbidden fruit. Doing something against what God has told you to do is a sin. Sin was introduced into mankind and now every person since Adam and Eve has been born into sin. God wants us to be without sin and He sent His Son Jesus to reconcile us back to Him. All you have to do is to believe in Jesus, who He is, and be baptized to be reconciled back to God. It begins with you wanting to connect back with God and confessing with your mouth (words) and believing with your heart the following:

Repeat these words, *"God, this is ___ (your name)*
_____. I have sinned against you. I am sorry. I love
you. I thank you for your Son, Jesus, whom you sent to save me
from my sins. I acknowledge Him and I acknowledge You, God.
Please forgive me. I thank you and I receive Your gift of eternal
life through Your Son, Jesus. Amen."

This starts the process of your new life with God and His Son Jesus and His Spirit the Holy Spirit. You need to connect with a Bible-based place of worship and begin your new life of growth and service to God. Let me be the first to congratulate you on your decision to make a connection with God. Consult with Him every day and let Him lead you along the life paths you will journey on and through. Prayer is just that, consulting with God. Talk to Him. Seek His advice and counsel and direction on what you need to do. God wants to see you prosper and do well; however, His way of doing things may not be the same way you would do things. He has a sense of humor and He is compassionate about His children. Talk, listen, obey and do. Talk to Him. Listen to what He tells you. Obey what He is telling you to do. Do those things by taking action. Some things might not be easy, but in the end, it will be worth it. He may not reveal to you the entire plan or all of the actions you will have to do at one time. He only gives you what you can handle at the moment. You may be impatient and want to know everything all at once. God does not operate like that. You have to trust Him and believe.

1. How would you grade the decisions you have made in this classroom of life so far? _____

2. What lesson(s) have you learned from that decision?

_____

_____

_____

_____

_____

_____

_____

CHAPTER 2: POWERFUL DECISIONS IN THE CLASSROOM OF YOUR FAMILY AND RELATIONSHIP LIFE

Teacher: Class, there are many types of relationships in life: dating, marriage, children, family, parents, and others. What types of powerful decisions will you have to make in the classroom of life for your relationships? There will be selecting a life partner, a permanent relationship, starting a family, and even new decisions if those initial decisions did not work out as you wanted them to.

First, a decision is the selecting a life partner. What type of person do you want to date? Do you know that there is a difference between dating and being in a relationship that has a future? It pays to know what you want from a mate and what are your deal breakers - those things you won't compromise on. Make a list. Your list will be personal to you. Don't just have things on your list that are physical requirements only – like height, weight, hair, facial feature, and body features. Be sure to list internal qualities that you want: character, trust, spirituality, work ethic, family, etc. Others, like your family and friends, may give you their opinions and suggestions, but only you know what you want and what you don't want. You will have to live with the decisions that you make. We live in an information age and you can find out about your mate from many sources, including asking them some very important questions to find out what you need to know first before making your selection. Some people make the mistake of not asking and not doing their research before making the final selection. Then you wake up afterward and wonder, "What did I just do?" Not doing your due diligence can lead to some unintended life-long consequences. You need to know how the other person feels about things like their career and work life, children, money, roles of the husband/wife in the relationship, and their spiritual life. Do any of their answers give you cause to be concerned? You cannot change the other person; you can only change Yourself! While every relationship requires some type of compromise, there are some things that you know that you will not compromise on. Again, you will not be able to change the other person. You can only change YOURSELF!

Look at your permanent relationship as a profitable business. What is the vision for this relationship? What are the goals for this relationship? What are some of the things that you want to accomplish in this relationship? Who will be responsible for which roles in this relationship? Who will ultimately handle which jobs/positions in this relationship? Will children be a part of this relationship? If so, how many and when?   Again, please have these discussions before you say, "I do."

Making the powerful decision to have children can be one of the most important decisions that a person and a couple can make. This is an awesome opportunity to have children, adopt, raise, train, care for, support, and be responsible for another human being.   Class, we will hear from three guests today who will share their Powerful Decision on Children and Family Relationships.

Teacher: Welcome to the three of you and thank you for sharing your Powerful Decisions concerning the family.   First, let's hear from Ms. Smithie Thomas Vaughn. Hello to you, Ms. Vaughn.

Ms. Vaughn   Thank you for having me.

Teacher: Tell us a little about yourself:

Ms. Vaughn: OK. I am a Marketing Sales Director at my company. I live in Georgia. I have an undergraduate degree and a master's degree.

Teacher: Thanks again for coming today. Tell us your Powerful Decision regarding your child.

Ms. Vaughn: I have a child. Being a mother and being serious about it, is the best experience in the world. I also decided to breastfeed my baby and I did it for 16 months. I learned that being responsible for another human being takes priority and you have to be unselfish, and that little person relies on you for everything.

Teacher: How old were you when you made the Powerful Decision to have a child?

Ms. Vaughn: I was 31 when I decided I wanted to be a mother, but I was 34 years old when I actually became a mother.

Teacher: What did you learn from making this decision?

Ms. Vaughn: I became a totally responsible person. I was consumed with making my son a priority and giving him everything he needed. His needs and loving him were my total focus.

Teacher: Did your life change from this decision?

Ms. Vaughn: Yes, my life changed and I was no longer just responsible for just myself but for this precious little person that God gave to me.

Teacher: Who do you want to thank for helping you to make this decision?

Ms. Vaughn: There were several people that I want to acknowledge. First, my goddaughter's mother, Ms. Hutchings, helped me to see how great motherhood was. Next, Ms. Fuller helped me to decide to breastfeed by showing me how wonderful it was. She had me read the book, **"The Womanly Art of Breastfeeding"** and that resource shared everything with me on how important it was, not only for the baby's nutrition but for bonding. As an older mother, that is exactly what I wanted to do.

Teacher: Wow. What areas of your life were impacted by this decision?

Ms. Vaughn: Every aspect of my life was impacted in a positive way. Watching my son grow, mature, and change into an adult is very fulfilling for me in the type of job I have done.

Teacher: Thank you again Ms. Vaughn for sharing your Powerful Decision. Class, let's show our thanks to Ms. Vaughn and her presentation.   Now, we will hear from Mr. Earnest Francis, Jr. and his Powerful Family Decision. Hello Mr. Francis, Jr. and thank you for coming to our classroom and sharing your Powerful Decision.

Mr. Francis, Jr.:   Thank you for the invitation.

Teacher: Tell us a little about who Mr. Francis, Jr. is.

Mr. Francis, Jr.:   I live in Texas. I graduated High School, with some college credit hours through my time in the military. After the military, I got a job with the United States Post Office.

Teacher: Tell us about your Powerful Decision.

Mr. Francis, Jr.:   One of the most important life decisions I have made was <u>not</u> putting my middle daughter up for adoption.

Teacher: Wow. What did you learn from making that decision?

Mr. Francis, Jr.:   What I learned from this decision was that God doesn't put too much on you that you can't handle. If you truly believe in Him and His awesome word that no weapon formed against you can prosper, then there is no obstacle or issue that you can't overcome or conquer!

Teacher: How old were you when you made this decision?

Mr. Francis, Jr.:   I was about 26 years old at the time.

Teacher: How did your life change from this decision?

Mr. Francis, Jr.:   I was blessed to be able to raise and still raising one of the most wonderful and amazing children on planet Earth! I cannot see myself living without her in my life. I know my life would have a huge void in it if we had proceeded forth with that adoption. She is a loving child, and naturally super, super smart. She has been making straight A's on her report card ever since she has been graded under the A, B system. She has made perfect scores on at least one subject on the end-of-the-year CRT tests since the 2nd grade. She loves to read and tells the best stories!

Teacher: Who do you want to thank for helping you to make the decision not to put your daughter up for adoption?

Mr. Francis, Jr.: I want to thank God first of all for forgiving me for my sins and my way of thinking back then. I want to thank God for blessing me with such a unique daughter. I would like to thank my dad, Earnest Francis, Sr., for talking me out of going through with the adoption. At the time I thought it would be a struggle because my oldest daughter had just been born about 1 year and a half before. I had just got hired on at the Post Office and I wasn't guaranteed any hours. God did what He always does. I got 40-plus hours every week and was bringing home between 60K and 70K roughly with overtime each year.

Teacher: Is there anything else that you would like to add?

Mr. Francis, Jr.: Yes, I would love to say that I love my Dad for encouraging me and letting me know face-to-face that if I went through with the adoption, I would be making a decision that I would regret the rest of my life. Each time we added a new addition to the family our income was enhanced by the grace of GOD. I have been honored and blessed to be my daughter's father.

Teacher: Thank you so much for sharing your Powerful Decision Mr. Francis, Jr.   Class, our next guest is Ms. Angela Christian.   Hello Ms. Christian.   Thank you for coming to our classroom and sharing your story.

Ms. Christian: Thank you for having me today to speak to your class.

Teacher: Tell us a little about yourself.

Ms. Christian: My name is Angela Christian and I live in South Carolina. I have a master's degree and I am currently working as a County Administrator for a local government.

Teacher: So, tell us about your Powerful Decision.

Ms. Christian: The most important decision that I have made is adopting my daughter.   For health reasons, I had a hysterectomy. I thought it was the final chapter after battling infertility and multiple miscarriages.   Even after a divorce, I still wanted to be a mom.   I embarked on a journey that would change my life as a 40-year-old single person. I took the classes

through the Department of Family and Children Services (DFAS).

They prepare you for the very worst if you adopted a child

through their agency. Early in the process, I decided to adopt

an older child. After the frustrations of all the bureaucracy

involved in adoption and the support of family and friends, I

picked up my 5-year-old daughter almost 2 years later who had

lingered in foster care most of her young life.

Teacher: What did you learn from this decision?

Ms. Christian: Faith and persistence will pay off. If I

had listened to the naysayers, I would never have completed all

the paperwork and processes necessary to adopt a child as a

single person. The process is time-consuming, costly, and

arduous. Fortunately, DFAS and a local law firm were able to

assist me with legal expenses to complete the adoption process.

The support of my family and friends through the process kept

me encouraged to the end. Even when I got a more demanding

job, there was support from family and friends. Friends and

family picked her up from daycare, took her on play dates,

tutored, and helped with homework when I had to work late. I learned that it takes a village to raise a child and you have to ask for help when needed.

Teacher: How did your life change from this decision?

Ms. Christian: When you step out on faith, God will see you through. I received a special gift - my daughter, and I am just the facilitator for her life. Now, she is a vivacious young adult that is well-adjusted and never meets a stranger. I hope the world is ready for her because she is destined for great things.

Teacher: Who do you want to thank for helping you to make this decision?

Ms. Christian: Family and friends and my current husband for believing in my vision.

Teacher: What areas of your life were impacted by this decision?

Ms. Christian: Her adoption reshaped the landscape of my life – I had a new purpose. Motherhood is worth all the sacrifices, tears, and joy. Often, folks will tell me how lucky my daughter is, but I believe that I am the lucky one because I get to mold and shape her life.

Teacher: What areas of your life were impacted by this decision?

Ms. Christian: My areas that were impacted include my financial, emotional, spiritual, and professional life.

Teacher: Thank you so much Ms. Christian for sharing your Powerful Decision with us. Class, let's thank Ms. Christian, Mr. Francis, Jr., and Ms. Vaughn for sharing their Powerful Decisions on having children. We are so blessed by each of your stories. Thank you all again for sharing. So, class, you can see, the powerful decision to have a child and what it can mean to your life is incalculable. Class, we are going to take a break now and when we come back we are still going to explore more Powerful Decisions in Relationships. We have some additional guests who will talk about their decisions as it relates to selecting a spouse, sacrificing for their children, leaving their family, and creating a meaningful relationship and family decision.

Teacher: Welcome back class. Did you enjoy the earlier guests? Now, I want to share some information on relationships. Do you know what kind of relationship you want? When you fail to plan for your relationship and fail to discuss those plans before making a relationship permanent, you could find out later that you and your partner are not on the same page. Each person can find themselves in a relationship that they did not intend and then they begin looking for a way out. Getting out can be both an emotional and a legal rollercoaster and can leave one or both parties with many scars.

Some people choose to enter into a pre-nuptial agreement/contract before making the relationship permanent. A pre-nuptial agreement is a contract between two people who are about to marry regarding their respective property and support rights if there is a termination of the marriage by divorce. Some people like pre-nuptial agreements and some people do not like them. Those who like them like the fact that it will eliminate any confusion and doubts about the distribution of property if things do not go as planned. Those who do not like pre-nuptial agreements could see them as an easy way out of a marriage. Having a signed contract may tend to show that there is no commitment to stay in the marriage and work it out. Usually, people enter into a pre-nuptial agreement, or even suggest it to the other party because the person has a considerable financial estate before entering into the marriage. They want to protect it from the other party, who usually does not have the same degree of financial estate if the marriage does not work.

If there is no pre-nuptial agreement on the front end and there is a legal divorce on the back end in case the marriage does not work out, it could be a nasty process. Divorce can be a mutual decision or it could be adversarial in nature. A judge or even a jury will make a determination of the division of assets, custody, and visitation of children, payment of spousal support and/or child support, and resolving all marital issues of the parties. No two cases are ever alike because no two people are alike and no two situations are exactly alike. Even if the parties agree and write out a joint agreement of how they want these issues to be resolved, it can still be reviewed and some parts of the agreement will not be honored. The Judge can still do something else, especially as it relates to issues of the children. Laws in each state do vary, but usually, as it relates to minor children, the Judge is going to do "what is in the best interest of the children" in making a legal decision. The amount of child support, even if the amount is an agreed amount by the parties, will also be reviewed by the judge to make sure that it is fair to the children involved. The husband and wife are adults and they can agree on anything that relates to them. Usually, the Judge is going to assume that adults know what they are agreeing to unless there is coercion among the parties. But on all issues that relate to the children, the Judge is going to look out for their interest and question any "agreement" of the parties to make sure that the agreement that relates to the children is fair and in their best interests.

In relationships where the parties just cohabitate and do not legally marry, the rules could be different to determine the division of property, child support, and other issues. Be sure to discuss your rights, obligations, and responsibilities with a licensed attorney in the state where you live to determine the legal ramifications of your situation. Legal issues that affect a child born in a relationship outside of marriage will be treated differently than a child born in a marriage. In a marriage, a child born to the parties is legally recognized to be the child of the mother and the father, unless there is legal evidence to challenge paternity allowed by the Judge in a court hearing. Outside of marriage, the paternity of the child has to be proven either by the agreement of both parties, the father signing the birth certificate, or with a paternity DNA test.

Legally and morally, both the mother and the father of the child are responsible for the financial support of the child. If the mother and the father are not living together, both still have a legal and moral responsibility to support their child. If one of the parents is absent from the household and not fulfilling that duty, then it could cause the custodial parent to seek financial

74

assistance to support the child from the state. There are also situations where the child is not living with either parent but is living with a third-party relative, a legal guardian, or in foster care. If that custodial parent or the non-parent custodian of the child applies for benefits from the state to assist with the financial needs of the child, additional legal actions will be initiated. If both the mother and the father are noncustodial parents of their child, both are responsible for support for the child. Legal action will be initiated against both noncustodial parents to secure financial support and repayment of the debt created by the custodial person who has received financial support from the state. Don't assume that you know what the law is in your state. Find out. Documentation and recordkeeping are key for both parties regarding what they did or did not do to support their child. Keep your receipts and your documentation intact.

Visitation rights with the child by the noncustodial parent can also be an emotional journey. Children need love and support and contact with both parents, unless the court has deemed it unsafe. Visitation is not tied to child support. One right is not dependent upon the other. Grandparents may also have to seek court action to exercise their visitation rights with the child, especially when one parent is deceased or when there is a breakup of the relationship or a divorce. Adults really have to exercise restraint and keep their emotions in check and put the interests of the child ahead of their own personal interests.

Spouses/mates and children are not the only relationships you have in life. There are relationships with your parents and other family members. You cannot pick your family. They are who they are. You can decide on the type of relationship you want to have with them. Your growth and development as a person are shaped by many things – your family, your environment, your friends, your exposure to things, and your decisions. Sometimes, your family can be a lesson of what not to do. You see what type of person your family members are and you make a decision not to be just like them.

Powerful Decisions in the Classrooms of Life

Teacher: So, class, we now have some guests to talk about their Powerful Decisions as it relates to the relationships with their family, their mates, and children's relationship with their parents based on how they grew up. Our first guest is Mr. T. Cole. Let's welcome him to the classroom.

Teacher: Hello Mr. Cole. Welcome to our classroom.

Mr. T. Cole: Thank you for the invitation to share my Powerful Decision.

Teacher: Tell us a little bit about yourself.

Mr. T. Cole: I live in California and I work as a business consultant. I also am ex-military with the Marines.

Teacher: Mr. Cole, tell us about your Powerful Family Decision.

Mr. T. Cole: The most important powerful life decision I've made thus far was when I declined to accompany other family members on a retaliatory drive, by shooting in a nearby town. It was particularly tough and frightening as the orchestrator was a family member, who had developed a reputation as an iron-fisted drug dealer in our small neck of the woods. I stood there almost numb watching him provide the other young guys with guns and nervously waited for him to get to me because how was I gonna say "no." He was about 6 years my senior, aggressive, and hot-tempered. I had to make a decision on the fly because I knew this could turn out badly. So, I mustered up the courage to tell him no. He rebuffed and told me to take the gun and get in the car. He became angry and began to challenge the burgeoning manhood I thought I had at that time. He then forced the gun into my chest and told me to get in the car. Again and I said no once more. Now, he's completely enraged, hurling expletives at me, and then he says that if I didn't take the gun and go that he was gonna pistol whip me with it. I was utterly terrified but boldly told him to do it if he must. Once he saw the fear and determination on my face, he just called me a punk and got into the car. I was left there with another older drug dealer who told me that I made the right decision.

Teacher: Oh my goodness Mr. Cole. I am sorry that that happened to you. What did you learn from this decision?

Mr. T. Cole: I learned the power of taking a stand for what you believe in no matter the consequence.

Teacher: How old were you when you made this decision?

Mr. T. Cole: I was only 14 years old.

Teacher: How did your life change from this decision?

Mr. T. Cole: I became a bit of a loner because the majority of the young men who got into the car were my closest cousins that I'd grown up with all my life. It became clear to me that we weren't gonna be the same again as they got into selling drugs and living that lifestyle. I was looked upon as a square. I knew then that I wanted to escape that environment and began to explore the options of college or the military as vehicles to make a better life for myself.

Teacher: Who do you want to thank for helping you to make this decision?

Mr. T. Cole: My great-grandmother was very supportive of me.

Teacher: What areas of your life were impacted by this decision?

Mr. T. Cole: I became more self-aware of the influence men can have and decided to be an example to my younger cousins and two nephews.   I learned that making good decisions and following your dreams can take you far away from the hell on earth that our poverty-rich hometown can be at times.

Teacher: Anything else about this decision that you want to share?

Mr. T. Cole: Not really, but I will say this. It is kind of sobering now that I think about where I am now and where all the other participants of that fateful night are now.

Teacher: Mr. Cole you truly made a Powerful Decision about your life and I am thankful that you made that decision for your life. We have been truly blessed with your decision and your ability to be transparent with my class. Thank you so much for sharing.

Mr. T. Cole: Thank you again for having me.

Teacher: Class, let's show our appreciation to Mr. Cole for sharing his Powerful Decision with us today. Thank you again, Mr. Cole.

Class, our next speaker is Retired Colonel George R. Fields. Let's welcome Retired Colonel Fields to our classroom. Tell us a little about yourself.

Powerful Decisions in the Classrooms of Life

Retired Colonel Fields: I live in Georgia. I have a master's degree in Human Resources/Management. I am a JROTC Instructor and an Entrepreneur.

Teacher: So, please tell us about your Powerful Decision.

Retired Colonel Fields: I would like to share two Powerful Decisions if you will allow me to.

Teacher: Absolutely Retired Colonel G.F. We would love to hear about both Powerful Decisions.

Retired Colonel Fields: The first one I want to tell the class about is my decision to make the Army a career and my second decision is deciding to get married.

Teacher: Ok, please tell us about these two Powerful Decisions.

Retired Colonel Fields: In both cases, they were absolutely the right decisions. Over my 28 years of Army service, I had numerous opportunities for personal growth and challenging life decisions. Equally fortunate in married life to have a partner that has helped me maintain a balance between my career, family, and outside Army interests.

Teacher: How old were you when you made these decisions?

Retired Colonel Fields: The military decision came very early when I joined ROTC while in college. I guess marriage was also early at the age of 24 after only knowing my wife for 9 months.

Teacher: How did your life change from these decisions?

Retired Colonel Fields: At the age these two decisions were made, I didn't see them as life-changing. But they both added clarity and focus on my future.

Teacher: Who do you want to thank for helping you to make these decisions?

Powerful Decisions in the Classrooms of Life

Retired Colonel Fields: The person that most influenced my decision to pursue a military career is retired Major General Walter P. Pudlowski. When I first met the general, he was serving as the Operation Officer for our Battalion. My interest was in sports medicine, but his observations were that I was definitely the person our country needed in the armed services. As far as deciding to get married, well that's on me having the courage to say hello after seeing my wife for the first time and then twice in one day.

Teacher: What areas of your life were impacted by this decision?

Retired Colonel Fields: The military creates so many experiences ultimately impacting life and death situations in war-based information I provided to senior leaders. Being in the room with some of the Army's top leaders as they briefed the Secretary of Defense on preparing sites for Presidential visits will be a lifetime memory. But all that pales in comparison to the numerous men and women I have served with, many of who will be lifelong friends.

As for my wife, I could not have a better partner as we have traveled a very long way together. Yes, we have had our share of highs and lows but growing stronger every step along the way.

Teacher: Is there anything else about these decisions that you would like to share?

Retired Colonel Fields: Life is about a purpose and there is no greater purpose than be in the service of one's nation. Equally, life is better lived with a partner that brings balance. Not all days will be perfect, but growing together with someone who is there for you makes life a much more pleasurable experience.

Teacher: Thank you so much Retired Colonel Fields for sharing those two Powerful Decisions. Thank you for your service to our country. Thank you for your example of leadership and being a devoted husband to your wife. It truly was love at first sight based on what you have shared with us. Again, thanks for sharing with the class.

Retired Colonel Fields: Thanks for inviting me to share with the class.

Teacher: Class, let's show our appreciation to Retired Colonel Fields for speaking to us today. Class, I hope that you are taking these presentations to heart and learning that each one of you will make Powerful Decisions about your life as well.

Class, our next speaker is Ms. L.S. Let's welcome her. Hello Ms. S. How are you today? Thanks for coming and speaking to our class about your Powerful Decision. Tell us a little about yourself.

Ms. L.S.:   Thank you for inviting me. I live in Georgia. I have completed some of my college education. I am married and a housewife. I also have 2 children.

Teacher: Again, welcome to our classroom. Tell us about your Powerful Decision.

Ms. L.S.:   When I was young, I thought I knew what was best for my life. I had in my mind the kind of man that I would date and one day marry. I had it all mapped out. I'm Mexican and always wanted a Mexican boyfriend. I visualized my Prince Charming, how he would look, how he would act, but that ideal man always ended up breaking my heart. I came to America when I was 21 by myself. I was on my own with no parents, and I was a little wild child. I set my own boundaries, but I broke many of them. I was independent at 100%. I was working multiple jobs and making my own money. There was no one to tell me what to do. I was renting a room from a friend. I was dating and partying all the time. I thought I was happy. I have my freedom. I was going to nightclubs Monday through Sunday. I would come home from work, take a shower, and then get ready to go out. It was a never-ending cycle of just going out every night, coming home, taking a little nap, eating, and going to work. That was my happiness, or so I thought. But then there was an emptiness on the inside. I kept so busy with working up to three jobs and always going out so that I would not think about being alone. When I come home I'd cry because I'll be sad and lonely. I was not respecting my body. I was depending on men to make me happy and I was just left broken-hearted. These men, who don't even treat you right, would just want you because they want a moment of pleasure.

I just kept up with this cycle of living. I would like to party. I was looking for a particular kind of man. He had to be Hispanic, had to speak Spanish because my English was so bad, had to be Catholic, and had to be someone who can dance. I never smoked, never drink, and never did any type of drugs. I never saw the need for it, but my need was just to go out and dance all night until my feet would be purple. I did not care. I just wanted to spend my days dancing the salsa and looking to be happy. I also wanted my man to be a good salsa dancer and look a certain way with those mysterious eyes. Usually, the men that

I dated looked how I wanted them to look, but every time I ended up heartbroken. I realized that I allowed that to happen to me. I would end up crying. I thought that there isn't a heart that loves me. I would wonder why God. Why me? But the cycle repeats and repeats and repeats.

But then it happened. I met my husband M.S. He was the opposite of what I thought I wanted. He was not Hispanic, not Catholic, and did not like to salsa dance. We met on a blind date. He had a beard. He was always dressed up. He has a quiet spirit. I am very talkative. I thought he was out of my league. But he was different from every man I had dated before. He listened to me. He made me feel different when we were together. He was really treating me in a special way and not trying to just have sex with me. But I kept him in the friend zone. Then about 3 months after we met, he asked me if he had a chance to really date me or if was he wasting his time. I knew that I had to be honest with him. I did not want to hurt his feelings or hurt him in any way because he did not meet my definition of my Prince Charming. I just didn't want to lose him. I didn't want him to leave my life ever. I talked to my sister and told her about M.S. She told me that I should give him a chance. She told me that maybe I didn't even know what it would be like to date him. She also said to me that I always look at the external person – how they look, their eyes, their body, how they danced, etcetera. But how does it always send? Give M.S. a chance. I took a couple of days to think about it. Then I decided to let M.S. know that I didn't want to lose him that I could be very difficult, and didn't want to hurt him. If he was willing to try then I was willing too. I am so glad that I did. I really fell in love with him. I could not see my life without him. I could see myself married to him.

Teacher: Ms. L.S. your story is a common story. We sometimes look at the external instead of the heart of the person we should be with in a committed relationship.

Ms. L.S.: Yes, but I had to learn the hard way that everything that looks good on the outside is not good for you on the inside. Then it happened. I met a man who was not Mexican. He did not like to do the things that I liked to do. He did not meet what I had on my list of who my Prince Charming would be. But there was something about him. Today we are happily married. We have two children. We have been married for 11 years and I am grateful to God that I did not marry a man like the one I thought I wanted.

Teacher: What did you learn from that Powerful Decision?

Ms. L.S.:   I learned that I could make a list of what I think is best for me as if God does not know best. But at the end of the day, God knows best. His timing is perfect and His ways are better than our ways.

Teacher: That is a great lesson learned Ms. L.S. How old were you when you made this decision?

Ms. L.S.:   I was 26 years old.

Teacher: Based on what you have shared with us already, I think I know the answer to this question, but who do you want to thank for helping you to make this Powerful Decision?

Ms. L.S.:   My sister. She told me that something different is not something bad.

Teacher: Is there anything else you would like to share with the class regarding your Powerful Decision?

Ms. L.S.:   Yes, I would like to share this. Most, if not every, female thinks that she knows what her "Prince Charming" will look like based on those things in her mind. We are only interested in our "Prince Charming", but we usually end up with a frog. You kiss so many fake "Prince Charming" men, but they were actually frogs. Then you meet someone who does not meet your definition of "Prince Charming" and you thought he was a frog. But he turned into your true "Prince Charming" and you find the love and happiness that you were looking for. Be open and look at the inside qualities of the man.

Teacher: I could not have said it better myself. Thank you again Ms. L.S. for sharing your Powerful Decision in finding your real, authentic "Prince Charming."

Class, our next speaker is Ms. Caroline Harvey Baker who will be sharing her Powerful Decision regarding her family. Ms. Caroline Harvey Baker welcome to our class and share a little about yourself.

Ms. Baker: Thank you for the invitation to share. I live in Georgia. I graduated from high school. My deceased husband and I were small business owners. We have 4 beautiful children. I am enjoying my retirement now.

Teacher: Great Ms. Baker. Tell us about your Powerful Decision.

Ms. Baker: I want to start talking about my life after coming out of high school. I wanted to go on to college or if I didn't go straight to college, I did want to at least take up some kind of trade that would further enhance my life after school. I didn't

93

get a chance to do what I really wanted to do. But I did meet a young man and he looked very ambitious. We talked about life and we decided to get married. After getting married, we had four wonderful kids. My husband did get a little bit of college but he stopped kind of early and went into business.

We started raising children. They all wanted to go on and do something with their lives. The oldest one wanted to be a lawyer. We did what we could to help them to reach what they wanted to do in life. So far they did just that. We were very proud of what they have accomplished and that helped me to feel a little bit better about myself not going on and getting more education for myself. But it all worked out beautifully. The children got their education and went to college. At home, we raised them the best way we could. So far they weren't very disobedient. We are happy with their accomplishments. That makes me at least feel that I did something right with my life.

Teacher: So, what did you learn from this decision that you made? Would you say that you sacrificed things that you wanted to do for your family?

Ms. Baker: Yes. Sacrifices were all worth it. Whatever happened, again it was worth it. Although it was good, we still had some rough spots. What they were able to do was that they kept their eyes on the prize. It made us very happy. They really made themselves happy because that was something I instilled in them - to at least make yourself proud of what you accomplish in life. Always keep God first. Stay in the church. Try to do something with your life to help someone else.   So, all of this has happened and so this was one thing about my life decision to try to be the best parent I could be. They followed my example and that helped them to get through life and to do something great. That gave me the feeling that I'd done something right. It has not always been easy, but it has worked out really good.

Teacher: Where did you get your parenting skills from?

Ms. Baker: From my parents. My mother used to sit and read the Bible to us. So far all of us might not have gone to college but we did pretty good with our lives from the example of our mom and father. That's what really made it all work out. They led a beautiful life in front of us. It wasn't easy for them but they tried to live in a way to let their light shine. And it did shine really good. They were always home. Daddy and mother were home raising us. Therefore, we had something to pass on to our children. So far it's been good.

Teacher: So, what did you personally learn from this decision of being a good parent to your children? What did you get from it?

Ms. Baker: Well, when you do your best, number one, you try to stay on the right road. You do not venture out into the world and live the right life in front of them. So, that is one thing that enables them to understand, and me too, that you reap what you sow. This is so powerful. This comes from a Bible verse that we used to hear a lot about. (Galatians 6:7), *"Do not be deceived,*

God is not mocked; for whatever a man sows, that he will also reap."

So far I must have done something right because they turned out really good. I'm not saying they are perfect. You know they had some rough bumps here and there, but that's what life is all about. Just do your best and stay with the Word of God. There was a certain Bible verse that my mother would always tell us. Proverbs 3:5-6 states *"Trust in the Lord with all of your heart, and lean not on your own understanding; In all your ways acknowledge Him, and He shall direct your paths."* This is something that will keep you in the right frame of mind. When you started feeling down, just go to that verse and read it. She always talked about it and told us always go there and it will keep us in the right frame of mind. That's some of what kept me going through life. Again, if you treat people the way you wanna be treated, you will come out successful.

Teacher: How do you think your life changed as a result of raising a family?

Ms. Baker: It's hard to say, but it changed for the better that I do know. It wasn't easy bringing them up, but they turn out well. Other people tell me I did a good job - me and my husband. I am not saying that we did everything by the book, I'm sure we didn't. But the main lessons that they needed, they got because you must live right before people. You can't tell them anything if you are not doing right. So, you gotta go by what you know is right and not try to tell them one thing while you do another. I can speak for myself that I always thought of that. At the beginning of my life whenever I had a bad day or I thought that I ought to do something another way, the right way always keep me in the right frame of mind.

Teacher: Who do you want to thank for helping you to make this Powerful Decision about raising your family?

Ms. Baker: Again, my parents were real good about it; but oh my mother, she was the one. She was the main one I could go to with anything. She would always talk to me. If I was having a problem with my husband, one of the children, or whatever it was, she would sit down and talk to both me and my husband. She would always try to tell you in a way that, when she gets through, you could see that she loved you. She was always gonna try to make it as plain as she could that if you do what the Lord expects you to do, then that's when everything will work out. But if you expect your children to go the good way and you are going the wrong way, that's not gonna work. So, I always tried to stay on the right path. That way, they saw that I did ok with my life, then maybe some of them will want to be just like me. I hope so. I hope that they will be better and have a better life than I had. But anyway I'm proud of my accomplishments in raising my four children. I think they have shown me that they were always proud of me. They might not be proud of all of the decisions that I have made, but they could see down the road that it was the right decision.

Teacher: Therefore, if you could look back at your 20-year-old self from where you are now, what advice would you give that person?

Ms. Baker: If I could look back to when I was a teenager or young lady or whatever, I would always say to myself first to believe that God will bring you through whatever He brings you to. He will see you through it. So that was the main thing. Sometimes, I would get kind of despondent. But when you pray and you got a praying mother, then you've gotten something to lean on. Because when she gets through praying and talking to you, then you can see that life just seems to be so perfect if you just believe. Believing is everything.

Teacher: Is there anything else you want to share with the class today?

Ms. Baker: Just trust in the Lord. Always put Him first and ask Him anything. You can pray to the Lord and He will show you whether you are going right or wrong. Just wait for your answer. That's what my mom always used to tell us. Just wait on the answer. Don't be too fast to think you got it when you don't. Don't ever just go your way. Always go the Lord's way and He ain't going to lead you wrong. Try to treat people the way that you want to be treated. All of them are not going to give you the same treatment, but you will reap what you sow. That is one good thing that I do know. It has happened in my life that the main person that gives you stones all of the time, just give them bread anyway and pray for them. Everything will work out. When you are young, you think differently. But as you get older, you grow in grace. The stuff that you have learned in your life will see you through. That's one fact. And I hope something that I have said, and those that know me, I hope that I've done something good in my life that they wanna pattern after because I also know we all have done something that we are not too proud of, but we always had something that put us on the right track and that's the Lord. Don't leave Him out. Always put Him first.

Teacher: Thank you so much Ms. Caroline Harvey Baker for sharing your Powerful Decision on raising your family with the class.   Class, we have one final speaker to share with us her

Powerful Family Decision. Let's welcome Ms. Marchelle Glover and can you share a little about yourself with us?

Ms. Glover: Ok. I live in Georgia. I have recently retired from my job. I have an undergraduate degree.

Teacher: Thank you, Ms. Glover. Tell us about your Powerful Decision that has had an impact on your life.

Ms. Glover: It all began in 1981 when I made the decision to enlist in the United States Air Force. It was a decision that I made to try and change how I felt about my life. I had flunked out of college after starting at the age of 17 and not being ready. I can almost remember the day that I decided to enlist in the military. When I flunked out of college, I was 18 years old and I remember feeling like such a failure. I remember feeling like I was gonna be stuck in life.   I remembered what a recruiter told me back when I was around 16 years old in high school. I worked at the Veterans Administration and it was in the same building where the recruiter for the Air Force recruiter was located. I remember him telling me about going into the military. I was living in Detroit, Michigan at the time.

Teacher: What did your parents think about your decision to go into the military?

Ms. Glover: My mom was a single mom. She was happy but concerned. She said that if any of her children could make it into the military, it would be me.

Teacher: How long did you stay in the military?

Ms. Glover: I stayed in the military for a little over six years. I was actually discharged from the military as a result of the incident where I killed my husband in self-defense due to abuse.

Teacher: I learned that life does not operate in a straight line. There are things we have to go through that we don't understand at the moment, but on the backside, you understand why some things were necessary. Sometimes, God does things to get our attention, but we ignore it.

Ms. Glover: God has to knock me out with an iron rod. The bat will not do the job. But surprisingly, I never really questioned God why things had to happen that way in my life. I never questioned why I was sexually assaulted. I never questioned any of that stuff. I don't even feel like I was a victim and, God never allowed me to feel like a victim. I just always felt like there was a purpose for everything I had to go through. Now I know why. The purpose has been made clear. I now have a non-profit outlet helping other women who have gone through what I have gone through.

Teacher: How did your decision about going into the military have an impact on your family life?

Ms. Glover: Well, for one thing, I am much closer to a lot of people I've met in the military than I am to my immediate family. God provided me with another family when I was in the military stationed in Germany, in Panama, and away from my biological family. It is so ironic that my mom and all of my siblings have moved here to Georgia since I've been here. I really only got to be a part of my mom's and my siblings' life's for the most part since I've been in Georgia.

I'm the only one for the most part who keeps in touch with my siblings on my father's side. I have 10 other siblings on my father's side and there were 7 of us on my mom's side. My father is now deceased. I met my father when I was 14 years old. I had heard about him but I didn't meet him until I was 14. I had a relationship with him that got stronger in the last few years before he died. But for the most part, I had a lot of resentment growing up. I was the only one without my father when I was growing up. My other siblings on my mom's side all had their fathers in their lives as they were growing up. I did not have that. Then I later learned that my father was a great father to all of my other siblings on my dad's side, except for me. I learned that he would have been close to me but my mom wouldn't allow it because of the man she was with at the time. I had a great deal of resentment for that. But I prayed about all of my life for me not to resent my mom. I really just felt that when

I got to my 50s that I could feel like letting everything go and forgive.

Teacher: Wow Ms. Glover. How did you get to forgiveness and what impact has it had on your life?

Ms. Glover: Forgiveness is not for them; it is really for you. God is so amazing and awesome. I told my mom how I felt about everything. I forgave her for everything. It was a process to truly love my mom. I had to deal with the past and what I was holding on to. I had to get past it and get free. I really wanted to get to a point where I could go to her and genuinely hug her and genuinely hold her. I prayed for being able to get to that kind of relationship with her. What was crazy to everyone else was when I was younger, everybody felt like I was my mom's favorite child. But she was basically favoring me because I didn't have what the other ones had – a father.

Teacher: Did you go into the military to escape your life back then?

Ms. Glover: It was a different outlet for me. I didn't share a lot about my life with others. People thought that it was just a career change. But now I have come full circle. I am now with my biological family.   My children are now around their grandmothers, aunts, and uncles. Even my grandchildren are around my family and they babysit the grandchildren. While they were not there for me, now they are around for them.

Teacher: You have truly come through a lot.

Ms. Glover: Yes, I have. You know who gets the praise for that. I was open to what He was saying and teaching me. I have always tried to learn from my past. Part of my learning is that I have always tried to help somebody from making some of the same mistakes that I have made.

I truly feel like God has used my life in so many different instances. So, I don't fault my late husband for the incident with him. I thank him more now for what I've been through. I am able to relate to others. When other women can talk to me about what they are going through and they feel comfortable sharing those things with me. God has been using me for a long time.

I really don't have a pretty story. For a long time, I felt ashamed of what I'd been through. But now I have a foundation that helps women who have gone through abuse. I have a book coming out. I will help others with my book and the steps to overcome life's challenges. My foundation is **Because I Am, Inc**. Its mission is to provide a safe haven for women and children from all over the United States, and to offer a fresh start in order to allow them to escape an abusive situation. We offer positive solutions and are a resource for economic, educational, and family empowerment for Black families within the Middle Georgia area.

Teacher: Thank you so much Ms. Glover for your information and how you have been able to overcome, grow, and help others. Class, let's thank Ms. Glover.

Homework for this classroom:

1. How would you grade the decisions you have made in this classroom of life so far? _____

2. What lesson(s) have you learned from that decision?

_____

_____

_____

_____

CHAPTER 3: POWERFUL DECISIONS IN THE CLASSROOM OF YOUR EDUCATION AND/OR CAREER LIFE

Teacher: There is a "**Date You are Born – Date You Die.**" We all have these three things. But what are you going to do with that **"dash"** in the middle? Will you be productive? Will you do nothing with the time you have been given? It is up to you. Almost every child has had the following question asked of him/her, "What do you want to be when you grow up?" We answered and said things like doctor, lawyer, teacher, police officer, businessperson, military soldier, professional athlete, entertainer, and many other things. But how do you decide what you will be when you grow up? If you make a decision, can you change your mind? Of course, you can. Since we are not born out of the womb with the skills and training to be in these professions, even with talent, you have to prepare yourself to become that person. It starts with making a decision based on facts and not just emotion.

Suppose you want to become a doctor, do you know why? What type? How long it will take? Where should you get the education and training? Why not talk to someone who is already doing what you want to do? Interview them and find out:

- What do you like about your profession?

- What do you dislike about your profession?

- How long is the formal educational process?

- How long is the practical educational process?

- Would you pursue the same career knowing what you know now? If not, why?

- What advice would you give to those who want to follow in your footsteps?

- Would you be a mentor to others who would like to pursue this profession?

- Could you also recommend other mentors?

- Would you have any volunteer or internship opportunities with someone who is already in your chosen profession so that they can get a realistic view of the profession and not the glamorized opinion of the profession?

Don't be afraid of change. Living in a technological society, change is one of the constants in life. New gadgets are being invented and the impact it has on the way we live and work is tremendous. Sometimes, you have to have several options for a career path or at least be willing to change. Sometimes, the change is not a voluntary one, but due to a change in the economy or a personal challenge in your life. Change can be good. Several people that I interviewed indicated that one of the most powerful decisions that they have made so far has been in the area of education and career. Some went to school pursuing one field and changed their minds due to changes in the global economy. Some have learned that it is better to pursue a passion than the money from some professions. Some pursue careers based on family and societal pressures instead of what will be a fulfilling career doing something that they love.

Teacher: Class, we have a panel of speakers who are going to share their powerful decisions in their education and careers. These graduates of the Education and Career Class of Life have used their power to make a difference in the lives of many people. Let's welcome to our class the following: Ms. Sonja Pemberton, Mr. Richard (Rick) Dunn, Sr., Ms. Karen Baker, Ms. Mary Christine Cagle, Ph.D, Mr. Tony Howell, and Mr. Reco McDaniel McCambry.

Teacher: Welcome to each of you. Please tell us a little about yourselves first.

Ms. Pemberton: I live in Georgia. I have a master's degree. I am a wife and a mother of three.

Mr. Dunn Sr.:   My name is Rick Dunn and I live in Georgia. I have a bachelor's degree in Journalism. I served as graduation coach coordinator in my local school district.

Ms. Baker: Ok. My name is Karen Baker. I live in Georgia. I have a master's degree and I currently work as a Senior QA Engineer.

Dr. Cagle: I live in Georgia. I have a Doctoral degree, a Doctor of Philosophy in Political Science. I am an Associate Director for Policy, Planning, and Communication at the Centers for Disease Control and Prevention.

Mr. Howell: I live in Alabama. I am an instructor.

Mr. McCambry: I live in Georgia. I have a B.S. in Industrial Engineering. I am an entrepreneur.

Teacher: Class, will you agree that we are in for an excellent discussion on their Powerful Decisions in Education and

Careers? So panel, tell us about your Powerful Decision and how old were you when you made your Powerful Decision.

Ms. Pemberton: One of the most important life decisions I've made thus far is the decision to follow my bliss in my career choice. I spent years pursuing opportunities that would be financially rewarding and not necessarily personally satisfying and enjoyable. What might be a better way to describe it is an ah ha moment. It's the moment when you evaluate what your life has been in the circle of life after 5 decades.   Since I've just recently made the decision I'm still learning from it. The one that was immediately learned was when you follow your bliss and opportunities began to arrive that support your journey. Here's what I learned and know now:

- In my 20s, I thought I knew everything; I was "grown" and free to do as I pleased!
- In my 30s, I realized I still had a lot to learn.

- In my 40s, I figured out how to play other people's games to make it, which also began my quest for authenticity and to question my true purpose in life.

- In my 50s, I realized it's all a fruitless game if you continue to play by other people's rules or live your life constrained by them!

I got the answer to the question of the 40s. Your true purpose is to figure out what your innate talents are and how you can use them in service to others. I asked myself these questions:

- What are you passionate about?

- When do you feel most alive?

- What makes your heart sing?

The key to getting the answer is to wait and listen and observe all that happens around you after the question has been asked. The answer can come in many different forms and from the most unlikely sources. I'd been getting messages for several years regarding my creative talents and dismissed them as people being "nice!" A couple of years ago, my husband suddenly became quite ill and I realized, firsthand, everything can change in an instant. So, I decided it was time to live the life I was meant to live not the one I thought I should! I was 55 years old when I made this decision. It really changed because I let go of the pressure to be someone that was not authentically me. Free to be me! I then realized my only purpose in life was to make the ultimate decision to discover my innate talents and use them! Everything else would take care of itself. It's amazingly freeing to be Dorothy, following the yellow brick road as the bricks appear, and creating and directing my own path to OZ!

Teacher: Next Mr. Dunn, your turn.

Mr. Dunn, Sr.:   My Powerful Decision in the area of Education and/or Career was deciding to return to college to get my degree after being out of college for 17 years. I was 37 years old when I went back to get my degree. It opened the door to greater employment opportunities. It also was a great accomplishment for my family as I became the first to graduate from college. All areas of my life were impacted. Education opens so many doors. It allowed me to increase my income, get leadership positions with various organizations, and it put me in a better position to better provide for my family. This decision really made it clear to me that having a college degree is vital for any Black man to move forward in this society. Education truly opens doors to the next levels in life.

Teacher: Next Ms. Baker, your turn.

Ms. Baker: My undergraduate degree is in business administration, management, and marketing support. My master's degree is in human resources management. Although none of my degrees are in the information technology industry, I did an outlook on life to see the way the world was going. It taught me to pay attention to what's happening around me and to be more intuitive about the world. Also, I have been BLESSED to stay employed in this industry. I was 25 years old when I made this decision. It has blessed me to be more independent, live on my own, and provide me with many things (not all) I need to survive. This includes a roof over my head, food on the table, a car to drive around in, and the clothes on my back. Many areas in my life were impacted by this decision including my home life, my family, my relationships, and my self-esteem because I became empowered. I was able to provide things for myself.

Teacher: Next Dr. Cagle, your turn.

Dr. Cagle: I decided during undergraduate studies at East Carolina University in Greenville, NC, to delay graduation for 1 year to enroll in a fellow's program that had me working for a federal government agency. The program offered the potential to secure a federal government job after completing the internship program and obtaining an undergraduate degree from East Carolina University. My parents were not supportive of my decision, because I was one of two grandchildren who first went to college. I told my parents the reason for my choice was I did not want to graduate from college without a job. I did ponder this decision because my desire was a career as a newspaper (print) journalist working for a major newspaper as a contributing writer or an editorial writer.

I remember one of my favorite Journalism instructors, Mr. Warren, told me that it was a good idea to pursue the internship. He also told me not to stay too long because a federal government job can become very secure and I would be unable to venture out to become the renowned journalist I thought I would destined to become. My decision was also based on my desire to come to Atlanta. I remembered reading about the Centers for Disease Control and Prevention (CDC) and I wanted to intern at that agency. However, there was not much of a choice in federal agencies, and CDC was not among my choices. So I selected an internship with the U.S. Forest Service, Southern Region, in Atlanta. Suffice it to say, I did make it to the CDC and have been tremendously blessed in working with such an amazing organization and achieving a senior leadership position.

I think what I learned is that it was the best decision at the time. I knew a lot of peers who graduated college and did not have a job. Do I regret not becoming a renowned print journalist, no? My writing and analytical skills have been used in my personal and professional life. When anyone needs to write a letter, email, or communication, they (my family and co-workers) will call me. Dr. Richardson, my advisor at Georgia State University, during my master's and doctoral program, always complimented me on my writing skills. I also published four articles in metro-Atlanta, Black-owned publications. I think I was 19 years old when I made this decision. I was in my junior year of undergraduate school.

Teacher: Next Mr. Howell, your turn.

Mr. Howell: My Powerful Decision was conquering the fear of change. I took a leap of faith to commence a new course in my life. I was only 27 years old, but I had to conquer the fear of change. I also learned a lot about myself in the process.

Teacher: Fear can be very debilitating. But someone once shared with me what FEAR really stands for – False Evidence Appearing Real. It appears in our minds and we have created this animal that we even feed called fear.

Mr. Howell: I agree Teacher. When I took the leap of faith to commence a new course in my life, new opportunities presented themselves that I did not previously know existed.   Personal growth and knowledge about myself came flooded in.   It does not even compare to what I thought I knew about myself prior to taking the leap. Every aspect of my life was impacted. Although my finances went down initially, my work and personal experiences increased exponentially. My finances did too.

Teacher: Next Mr. McCambry, you are next.

Mr. McCambry: I started my own business at age 20 and I never quit. With faith and hard work, anything is possible. I became a better person and as a result, I began to get better results in my life. I truly want to thank God   and   those   who encouraged me to not give up on my dreams. Many areas of my life were impacted by my decision to start my own business including financially, socially, mentally, and so many other areas.

Teacher: Wow, thank you to each one of you for sharing. Is there anything else about your Powerful Decision that you all would want to share with the class? Anyone can respond to this question in any order.

Mr. McCambry: There are so many stories to support my Powerful Decision that detail how making this decision impacted not only my life, but thousands of others as well. I am a firm believer that one decision you make can drastically impact the rest of your life. And because of my decision, I'm not only able to live a blessed life, but able to pay it forward greatly!

Dr. Cagle: I increased the trust I have in myself with the Powerful Decisions I have made about my life. I knew that I would always be a very determined, independent woman. I knew that for all I would achieve, I would work for it myself, and that today makes me very proud.

If I could, there are a few people that I would like to thank for helping me. They include my East Carolina colleagues - Mr. Warren and Ms. Karen Thompson; the Financial Management Office administrative staff; the Counselor for the Internship Program; and last but not least my Uncle Walter (Pete) Cagle. He co-signed a loan for me to establish myself in Atlanta, and he never had to pay for any of the loans; I paid it in full. I am also most grateful to my Uncle Pete because of his tremendous support during my years at East Carolina University and who attended my graduation. He was supportive not only in love, but in support of using his car- he never trusted anyone else, and providing me with food from his pantry. Thank you all.

Mr. Dunn, Sr.: I also would like to thank two individuals, Dr. Claude Burnett and Micky Roberts for their support and encouragement to help me complete this goal of obtaining my college degree.

Ms. Baker: I also want to thank first and foremost, God, my creator. Then I would like to thank my family and friends who encouraged and challenged me. I would also like to share this with the class. Even though I made a good choice, I can't get too comfortable! Always follow your intuition!

Ms. Pemberton: All areas of your life are affected on some level when you are happy with who you are! The most impacted area of my life has been finances. It takes time and money to build a business successfully. The other area impacted was my confidence and belief in myself and my talents. I wake up every day loving my life a lot more! Life is truly a circle. I realize I'll never know it all and am continuing to experience each day with the wonder of a young child. We all need to go back to our 5-year-old selves! Seeing the world through the eyes of a child is a wonderful experience. At 5 years old, most of us believed anything and everything was possible, and it is! Let go and BECOME authentically you! Life becomes just as Forrest Gump said, "Life is like a box of chocolates, you never know what you're going to get!"

Teacher: Again, thank you to each one of our panel speakers today.   You all really shared a lot of valuable information. That included dealing with fear, not quitting on your goals, looking at internships, and examining the future trends in work professions.

Class, we have some additional guests who will share their Powerful Decision on Education and/or Career. Let's welcome our next speaker, Mr. Melton Torbert. Welcome to our class and please tell us a little about yourself.

Mr. Torbert: Thank you for inviting me to speak to your class. I live in Alabama. I have a master's degree in Human Resource Management. I am currently an Operation Support Specialist.

Teacher: Thank you and please tell us about your Powerful Decision in the area of Education and/or Career.

Mr. Torbert: Before I tell you about my decision, I am so concerned about this younger generation. They really have to take their education seriously. They have everything at their fingertips with their cell phones. They can look stuff up and play games. But they have to take their education seriously. This pandemic of 2020 and 2021 is going to have a serious impact on education. They are getting further and further behind. The parents are working or they are at home but not fully equipped to teach their children. The children can play video games on their computers, but act like they can't learn on the computer. I am just so concerned about the young generation.

Now, let me tell you about my Powerful Decision in the area of education. When I was younger, I decided when I was in 12th grade that I did not want to attend college. This was a bad decision. After high school, my counselor, Mrs. Emma Brantley, encouraged me to go to college. But I didn't attend college for one year after graduating. I worked full-time on the 3rd shift for one year in a tedious dirty job in manufacturing. I learned the hard way that the lack of education lessens your opportunities. So, I made a better Powerful Decision. I began to work on my education. One year later, I changed departments and started attending Southern Union Community College on 3 different campuses in 3 different cities in the early1980s. I attended day classes and night classes, depending on my work schedule. I even met my future wife at Southern Union. After graduation, I enrolled at Troy University in Montgomery, Alabama, taking night classes, and arriving back home at 10 p.m. After completing my bachelor's degree, I was accepted into Troy University Graduate Program again continuing night and weekend classes.

Teacher: What did you learn from that decision to continue your education?

Mr. Torbert: I learned that education + knowledge = power! Education can and will afford one opportunities and many possibilities for a better lifestyle and social economics. After 13 years at my 1st full-time job, I was laid off from my company. I had only 2 or 3 classes before getting my master's degree. I was not going to stop. My son was 6 months old when I was laid off. But it was a personal gratifying decision to complete grad school. My wife and I even started preparing for our children's college fund when they were very young. We knew how pertinent and imperative one's educational achievements are in life. I would constantly tell my children about the need to continue their education.

Teacher: Who do you want to thank for helping you to make this decision?

Mr. Torbert: My late mother was my biggest cheerleader growing up. She was truly a big supporter. After marriage, my wife was a big supporter of my completing grad school. I have been very fortunate and blessed. I tell my children and young people in general about the struggles I had working and going to class. There were no online classes back then.

Teacher: Is there anything else you would like to share with us?

Mr. Torbert: Both of my children were blessed and earned many scholarships to attend Auburn University and Troy University for their undergraduate degrees and they stayed on campus or in apartments. They got the full experience. Both children then earned master's degrees from Georgetown University and Alabama. I shared my story with them on the importance of education. I share with other young people as well. Education is key.

Teacher: Thank you so much, Mr. Torbert. I agree wholeheartedly with your talk on the importance of education. It is truly a key to a better life. Class, join me in thanking Mr. Torbert.

Class, our next speaker is Mr. JL Harvey. Let's welcome him to our class to share his Powerful Decision in his career. Please Mr. Harvey tell us a little about yourself.

Mr. Harvey: Sure. Thank you for inviting me to speak to your class about my Powerful Decision. I was born in Alabama and I now live in Georgia. I was drafted into the military as a young man. I grew up on a farm, and I was a businessman as a brick mason. I am now retired. I will start with my life when I was coming up as a young child growing up in the country of Alabama, down in the field. I always wanted to have something of my own. I had me a little farm down there behind the house. While my other siblings were resting, I would be working my little farm. They used to call me "Farmer Brown". That was the name that they gave me, "Farmer Brown".

Teacher: How old were you when you were called "Farmer Brown"?

Mr. Harvey: I could've been no more than about 8 or 9 years old. My dad put me in the field plowing the field. He had to cut the plow handles for me to be able to reach them and use them. When I got big enough to actually plow and farm, I made more money on my stuff than my dad made on his. After we moved to another part of Alabama, I cleared up a new plot of ground and I again made more on my plot than my dad did on his. I was growing some of everything that my dad was growing on his - corn, watermelons, peas, and peanuts. I never raised cotton though like my dad did. I did have potatoes too on my little farm.

After my education, I went into the service, in the army. I got drafted into service in 1953. I had my basic training in Augusta, GA at Camp Gordon. They sent me over to Korea. I spent about a year in Korea. When I got out of the military, I started training in brick masonry. I took an 18-month course in brick masonry and another 18-month course in radio and TV.

When I finished the training, I went all out for the brick masonry. Mostly, I was working for myself; but I did work for another company the first year. I was working in Huntsville, AL, and I worked for another company for 1 year. That was 1965. Then in 1966, I went to Auburn and Opelika, AL, and I was working for myself. It lasted a long time until I semi-retired about 12 years ago in 2003 or 2004. I still did some small jobs on my own.

Teacher: How did that decision of starting your own business change your life?

Mr. Harvey: Well, it changed me a whole lot. I experienced a lot. I was able to help a lot of people, including myself. I made a decent living. When I was in the service, I was in communications. I was in a signal corp. I thought that I might have got a job with some major companies; but when I got out of the army in 1955, they did not have any people of color working in those companies. I even applied for jobs in civil service in the communication field. They were not hiring too many people of color either. So, I got into brick masonry. It was hard work and dirty work. I got interested in brick masonry because the job paid pretty well.

Teacher: If you don't mind me asking, how old are you right now?

Mr. Harvey: I am 89 years old.

Teacher: So, you are 89 years old now. Knowing what you know now about what all you have been through, what advice would you give to a person in their late 20s or early 30s who wanted to go into business?

Mr. Harvey: I would tell them to try to be the best in their type of business, be honest, and be fair. The main thing is to be dependable. My daddy used to tell us when we were coming up to let your word be your bond. I remember those words when I was in business.

I remember this one event I had when I was in business. I was to go to a job and close a foundation. The carpenter and the contractor were waiting on me to come up one evening. It got late in the evening. The contractor told the carpenter that I said that I was going to come up there and close up the foundation. It is late and I don't think that he is going to show up. But the carpenter said, didn't he say that he was coming? The contractor said yeah. Then the carpenter said then he is coming if he said he was coming. My word is my bond.

I had a lot of people would say to me that it was the hardest thing to get me to say that I will do something. Because they knew that if I said I was going to do something, they could be at ease because I was going to do what I said. If something came up, I would call and explain if I could not be there. Being dependable is one of our biggest assets. You have to be dependable these days and times. People have to be able to count on you.

Teacher: Mr. Harvey who made an impact on your life when you were growing up?

Mr. Harvey: There were different people, but mainly, my mother and father, sisters and brothers, and friends. They always encouraged me. They had a great impact on my life.

Teacher: Thank you Mr. Harvey for sharing the Powerful Decision made in your career with our class. Being dependable and making sure that your word is your bond are key points to have when you are in business.

Mr. Harvey: Again, thank you for the opportunity to share.

Teacher: Class, let's welcome our next speaker, Ms. Carolyn Dickerson. Thank you for coming and sharing your Powerful Decision in your career with our class. Tell us a little about yourself.

Ms. Dickerson: Thank you for the invitation to speak to your class. I live in Georgia. I have a master's degree and my current occupation is working as a Senior Instructional Designer.

Teacher: Thank you, Ms. Dickerson. Please share with us your Powerful Career Decision.

Ms. Dickerson: I want to talk about risks. When I was about 30 years old, I moved to a new city away from my family and friends. I only knew two people when I moved to this new city. I was a single parent of a 16-year-old. Taking a risk can be scary, but this is how you become sure you can make it with no safety net. I gained more self-confidence during this journey. I have a very large family and I always had support. However, on my own, I had to learn how to figure things out. I was from Maryland and had never been further than Virginia. I had a job that was ok, but I moved to try my hand at something new. I had opportunities I never thought were possible. I traveled and made friends outside my race - for the first time. I got comfortable with myself, got my daughter through high school and college, and found a church home. Oh, and the love of my life found me. Taking a risk can be scary, but this is how you become sure you can make it with no safety net.

Teacher: What did you learn from taking risks?

Ms. Dickerson:　　　　I would say that the biggest lesson was that I gained more self-confidence. Like I said earlier, I have a very large family and I always had their support. On my own, I learned how to figure things out. I feel like I would have stayed on autopilot if I had stayed close to family.

Teacher:　　　Who helped you make this decision?

Ms. Dickerson:　　　　A close friend encouraged me to try moving to another state. I did not tell anyone until the details were worked out because I knew they would try to talk me out of it. I had the same friends since 5th grade. I had to learn that you can find a community again. This time, I pick a community based on where I wanted to go versus where I had been. This changed my perspective on life and my ease with getting to know different "types" of people.

Teacher:　　　Wow, this is great. Is there anything else that you would like to share with the class?

Ms. Dickerson: Just go for it. I am happy I did it and I would do it again. But it was not always easy. It did cost me something, but it was not wasted.

Teacher: Thank you Ms. Dickerson for sharing this Powerful Decision with us on taking risks. Class, let's welcome our next speaker, Ms. Agnes C. Thank you for coming to speak to our class. Tell us a little about yourself.

Ms. C.: Thank you for the opportunity. I live in Georgia. I have a master's degree in Religious Leadership with an emphasis on Ministry with Youth. I am currently a Teen Ministry Coordinator.

Teacher: Again thanks Ms. Agnes C. and please share your Powerful Decision in the classroom of Education.

Ms. C.:   My journey began in the midst of being unemployed, dealing with constant foot pain with swelling, and realizing that I had previously decided **NOT** to further my education, I found myself applying for graduate school. I didn't apply to any ole graduate school. I applied to the Candler School of Theology at Emory! This might not seem like anything major to most people, but this was not the case for me.

As I mentioned, I had no intention of going back to school because I felt my days in a classroom were over. However, there was a "Spiritual prompting" that would not cease. My determination **NOT** to preach led me to explore other options and various colleges. Again, I was "prompted" to examine the programs offered by Candler. A very nice young man explained their Religious Leadership program and gave me an application, an information package, and a college catalog. I informed him that I didn't need any of those things because I didn't have the money to attend school, nor did I have the desire to start. I thank him for the information and left.

The leaders at my church decided to restructure the nursery, children's, and teen ministries. I was asked to work with the Teen Ministry. After about three months, I realized I was not equipped to handle their biblical questions, personal concerns, and problems. One month before the deadline, I began requesting recommendation letters, college transcripts, and writing essays in hopes of being admitted to Emory University's Candler School of Theology.   My faith was elevated to a totally different level when my application and everything were delivered by the deadline, despite having to address unexpected obstacles. Best of all, I was accepted into the Candler School of Theology and given a partial scholarship to help with my expenses.

Teacher: What did you learn from this decision?

Ms. C.:   I learned several things from this decision, but the most important thing for me was realizing that God will see me through any obstacle when I am doing what God has called me to do. I never even considered applying to Emory because I felt I had no possibility of being accepted. My college transcript was not something of which anyone could boast. Nevertheless, I am now a graduate of Emory University.

Teacher: How old were you when you made this decision?

Ms. C.:   I was about 58 years old.

Teacher: How did your life change from this decision?

Ms. C.:   Becoming a student after having taught for more than twenty years and being out of the classroom for almost ten was a drastic change. Learning to use the technology, and becoming familiar with the educational and religious jargon, so I could interpret the assignment and complete it. Despite this, the biggest change can be noted in my perspective about people. I never realized how narrow-minded I was before starting the journey to earn this degree. It should be noted that my perspective is still evolving.

Teacher: Who do you want to thank for helping you to make this decision?

Ms. C.:   First, I want to thank God for making this educational journey possible. Next, I want to thank my wonderful husband, Ernest, for being understanding, supportive, and encouraging. He never complained when I had to spend hours away from everything studying, completing assignments, meeting with other people, etc. Finally, I want to thank two other people. My sister Jackie is one. I thank her for believing in my abilities when I couldn't. She "spoke" success over my life and into my future. The other person is my friend Barbara. During the final hours, I had to complete an essay for the admissions application, I thought my time was up and I had missed the deadline. I was panicking. I called Barbara - almost in tears and explained my situation. She dispelled my fears, prayed for me, and told me to deliver my paper because everything would be just fine. Things worked out just as she predicted.

Teacher: What areas of your life were impacted by this decision?

Ms. C.:   For a time, all areas of my life were impacted because of the changes associated with the rigor of working on a degree. Now that I have finished and things are back to normal, I am trying to decide what's next. As some may say, "I'm all dressed up with no place to go."

Teacher: Anything else about this decision that you want to share?

Ms. C.:　　　　This decision revealed so many things about me. I thought this degree would prepare me to develop for youths an interesting, adventurous, insightful religious program that would introduce Jesus to some and deepen the faith of all. As I think about it, my decision to attend graduate school allowed me to really see myself – the good and the not-so-good. The various books, articles, lectures, and videos were the primary resources used to earn my degree, but the overall experience provided my true education. ***"To know thyself is the beginning of wisdom."*** Socrates.

Teacher:　　　Thank you so much Ms. Agnes C. for sharing your Powerful Decision with us. All of these powerful decision makers have shown why they are leaders in their respective careers.

Class, it is time for your homework:

1. What have you learned that can help you where you currently are in the Classroom of Education and/or Career?

    _____

    _____

_____

_____

_____

_____

_____

_____

2. What are the next powerful steps in your journey?

_____

_____

_____

_____

_____

_____

_____

_____

_____

_____

CHAPTER 4: POWERFUL DECISIONS IN THE CLASSROOM OF
YOUR HEALTH AND WELLNESS LIFE

Teacher: Making a powerful decision in all of the other areas of your life means nothing if you don't take care of your body and health. If you don't exercise, eat properly, and get plenty of rest, all of your hard work could be for naught. We have become a society of overweight individuals due to a lack of physical activity and proper diets. Some of the foods that we eat are full of chemicals and hormones that are having a negative impact on our bodies. You have got to move your body and break a sweat to work the most important part of your body, your heart. If you do not take care of your body, you will have challenges in the health department. How many days do you exercise for at least 30 minutes? How much water do you drink on a daily basis? How much living food: fruits and vegetables do you eat at each meal? If your answers are surprising you, then it's time to make a more powerful decision to take care of the one body you have been given. Everyone can do something to take care of their health. When was the last time you had a physical? Do you do personal body checks for changes to your body? Do you have a physician that you feel comfortable discussing what is going on with your body? The sooner things are detected, often the better for you. There are many options for treatment for your condition from traditional to holistic to experimental treatments.

Class, we have a panel of guests who are going to share their powerful decision in the area of health and wellness. When life throws you a challenge or obstacle or bumps in the road, how will you respond? We have Ms. Denise Troutman Holden, Ms. Marilyn Kenoly, Ms. Arleathia Chambliss, and Ms. Shari Moreira. Thank you ladies and welcome to our classroom. Let's begin with Ms. Denise Troutman Holden. Please tell us a little about yourself.

Ms. Holden: I live in Atlanta, Georgia. I have a bachelor's degree in Human Resources Management. I am a Wellness and Empowerment Coach.

Powerful Decisions in the Classrooms of Life

Teacher: Please share with us the Powerful Health and Wellness Decision.

Ms. Holden: One of my most important life decisions was relocating from Atlanta, GA to Dallas, TX in December 2007 for a HR Management position within the company I was working for.   It was a wonderful position that allowed me to become a HR Manager for several facilities in the Dallas area. I would be the only African American holding that position within the company.   I had never relocated anywhere alone before but I had always been intrigued with Dallas, TX. My daughter had just graduated from high school, so it was the prime time for me to make the move.   I relocated to Dallas alone and my daughter stayed in Atlanta and moved in with her dad and stepmom.

Relocating to a new city where I didn't have any friends or family was challenging but fun at the same time. It helped me to grow stronger as a person and as a woman.   I learned to become more self-sufficient and learned quickly how to find the resources I needed very quickly.   I, also for the first time in my adult life, had an opportunity to focus on my needs and wants first.

I was 50 years old when I made the decision to relocate. I enjoyed being on my own and spending time alone. It was so nice knowing that my day-to-day decisions were based on things that I wanted to do and things and places I wanted to explore. I made new friends and did a lot of regional traveling while I was in Dallas. I had a blast. While making the decision to relocate was not easy because I wanted to ensure that my children, family, and friends would support me in this decision. Overall, most did support my decision; my youngest child and best friends encouraged me to go and "explore my world" and I am so glad I did.

I ended up living in Dallas, TX for 3 years, and then my position was downsized. This was perfect because my goal was never to stay there any longer than 5 years. I was blessed to have received a large severance package which made it easy to relocate back home to Atlanta. When I returned to Atlanta, I decided to focus on my weight and health and started working out every day. I decided to wait a while before exploring my next employment opportunity.   After losing 15 lbs., I noticed a lump in my breast during self-examination and it was later diagnosed as breast cancer.   I strongly feel that it was a blessing that I was able to relocate to Dallas and eventually come back home with a severance package.   The money allowed me to not stress about finding working but rather focus on my health.   I am not sure if I would have found the lump if I had stayed in Dallas. The lump had not been detected on any of my previous mammograms.   I believe my weight loss allowed me to be able to feel the small lump.   I have spent the past 2 ½ years battling breast cancer.   I have had a mastectomy, chemo treatments, and reconstructive surgeries.   I am now a cancer-free survivor.   Moving to Dallas allowed me to grow personally, professionally, and financially. It also helped me to prepare for one of the biggest journeys of my life... overcoming breast cancer."

Teacher: Thank you so much, Ms. Holden. Next is Ms. Kenoly. Tell us your Powerful Health Decision.

Ms. Kenoly: Thank you first for having me here today and allowing all of us the opportunity to share our Powerful Decisions. I live in Vinings, Georgia. I have a bachelor's degree in Sociology. I am currently a Chief Information Officer.

In 2009, I faced a health challenge that caused me to make the most important decisions in my life. I lost my sleep for 2 years! Yes, I had chronic insomnia for 2 years. The decision that I made about this challenge was to find a natural solution to get back to sleeping normally without pharmaceutical drugs. What I learned from this challenge was to accept my intuition to trust that I would find a natural solution because I did not want to take sleeping pills or anti-depressants to sleep nightly.

I was 52 years old when I made this decision. My life became a living nightmare while in the process and financial disaster plagued recovery. It took doctors and a naturopath to resolve my issues and I now sleep naturally without drugs.

I would like to thank Almighty God and my mother for helping me make the decision. I trusted that natural solutions would be revealed to me and/or my doctors. I was referred to an ob-gyn who specialized in anti-aging. She believed in combining allopathic medicine with natural medicine, and I was referred to an excellent Naturopathic doctor with a specialty in traditional Chinese medicine and biofeedback.

As a divorced mother of a 15-year-old sophomore high school student, the financial impact was most devastating because natural solutions are not covered by medical insurance. I used all of my savings, 401k, and disability insurance to survive the disorder. The baby boomers will be the largest group of human beings going into menopause and andropause in the history of mankind. The chronic insomnia I experienced was due to entering perimenopause and my hormones, as well as vitamins/minerals, became EXTREMELY imbalanced. It was an experience I would not wish on my worst enemy. We need our sleep; sleep is how our tissues heal and our mind rests. As a result of my experience, I penned *"Wide Awake"* and I share it with insomniacs all over the world. It is my gift, my testimony, and my hope that the class will find something in my experience that will help them recognize their symptoms and find a solution to their challenge. I would like to offer this book to the class and you can find it at http://www.calameo.com/read/001398074566af1fd5193?authid=6QKswjvaN0ug.

Teacher: Thank you so much Ms. Kenoly for the book. Class, our next speaker is Ms. Arleathia Chambliss. Welcome, and please tell us about your Powerful Decision.

Ms. Chambliss: I live in Decatur, Georgia and I have a master's degree. I am currently a Senior QA Engineer. I would like to share two powerful decisions that have had an impact on my life. One is in the Career classroom and the other is in the Health classroom. However, both decisions are intertwined.

I believe that the most powerful decision I have ever had to make is to immediately resign from my career as QA Lead from a job I was blessed with after an 8-month layoff from another company. I had only been at the job for 3 months, but this job was so stressful and unorganized. I was working over 40 hours a week, doing 5-6 different assignments including the position I was hired to do. I was asked daily to attend 4-6 meetings a day, lead a team of 6 individuals, retested or triaged support tickets, create a test plan for bi-weekly release calls, prioritize workstreams, test case reviews, my own bi-weekly sprint work, and other team-lead administration duties. My days started at 7 a.m. in the mornings until 6 p.m. in the evenings. After 6 p.m., I spent catching up on the sprint work assigned to me personally with 2-3 day target dates. The company had no documentation. Each meeting I had to record each in order to replay to understand the enhancement and understand what was expected of my team. Most of my training was one hour of learning by doing. I constantly had to ask questions and inquire about the tools I needed to get the job done. The CTO - Chief Technology Operations - was always screaming at the teams to get things done. Everyone was stressed due to limited resources and unrealistic expectations from the CTO.

All of this caused me to become stressed and overworked. I begin to worry about meeting deadlines, pleasing others, and not having the tools I needed to do my job. I would express my concerns to my manager, but he would always say "we don't have time to create processes" or "this is what the CTO wants." I began to feel unworthy like my 20 years of experience were useless, asking myself how have I gotten this far in my career and unable to handle this pressure. My fiancé and I are building a house, and getting married soon. I felt like I needed to keep this job to help with the finances for our future. Due to COVID-19, I'm thinking I should stay put because of the job market. I felt like I would lose my relationship if I quit my job. I started to think I would be a failure. This started anxiety and insomnia. I would pace the floor at night, not sleeping, and not eating. My family noticed I would sit in my office 12-16 hours a day neglecting them and I had no personal life.

The last straw was when I began to have chest pains and no sleep. I started going through early menopause during which the stress elevated my anxiety. I was given an anti-depressant to keep my mind from wandering. I took it for 3 days and felt worse. I stop taking it and I felt better. I had to determine if all this was the stress from the job or just the process of me going into early menopause. I concluded it was the stress of the job.

I made the decision to leave the job. I learned from this decision that my health comes first. I can't worry about what the staff thinks of me leaving the job, because I will be replaced. I was 48 years old when I made this decision. My life feels better already. As soon as I heard my director thanking me for my service at the company, it was a load lifted. I have been sleeping and enjoying life. I have given myself some time before looking for another position to make sure I am truly okay. Plus, my mom was genuinely concerned about my behavior and didn't want me to be depressed and stressed by keeping her worried about me.

I would like to thank God, my mom, my sisters, and my fiancé for believing that something wasn't right about this job and encouraging me to know that the job was not healthy and was changing who I was. Mental health is a scary disease. Experiencing just a small portion of it gives me a new perspective on what people are going through. I cannot and do not want to imagine myself experiencing this ever again.

Teacher: Wow Ms. Chambliss. Your story is so powerful. A lot of us, especially women, juggle the demands of the work and sometimes to our detriment. Thank you for sharing your powerful decision. Class, our next speaker is Ms. Shari Moreira. Welcome to our class Ms. Moreira and please tell us about your Powerful Health and Wellness Decision.

Ms. Moreira: I also want to thank you for the opportunity to share my Powerful Health and Wellness Decision with your class. I live in Lawrenceville, Georgia. I attended community college and I am currently a customer service representative.

I was wondering why I was having uncomfortable monthly menstrual episodes and I finally went to my gynecologist, who sent me to a specialist. The specialist discovered that I had fibroids that were big as a grapefruit. This was in 2021. I had the decision to make if I wanted to hysterectomy and I am 52. I already have two kids, ages 13 and 24. I am done having kids, but I wanted to keep my body parts. My doctor referred me to one of her peers who was only interested in doing the hysterectomy. I never called him. I went to get a second opinion. My dad had also mentioned something about a different procedure to treat fibroids. It is a procedure where they would insert a type of catheter inside of you and it fights off the fibroids. It weakens and kills the fibroid. So, I made the decision to get that procedure done. It was noninvasive. I was put to sleep for this procedure. I did take awesome time off for about six weeks from my job even though it was from home. I just rested up. Initially, I felt like I just had a pregnancy. But I would do it again if I had to. I would not go the way of removing organs if you don't have to. It was a big decision to make and it was almost over a $30,000 decision though. My insurance paid a good portion of the costs and I had to pay a portion as well. I will have a follow-up MRI, but I just feel healthy now.

I just feel like I got something foreign out of my body. I do my research now. I do speak to people who tell me about their fibroids. I try to help them decide not to have everything disappear you don't have to. I tell them about my experience. But what I also look back on is what caused it. I'm doing more research. It's mainly African Americans who have it. I speak to African American females and other cultures about my experience. I was literally in a lot of pain on the left side of my hip. I went from not knowing the cause to now knowing it was the fibroids. I want to educate people and keep learning more about the cause of fibroids. I still have a follow-up with my doctor, who wanted me to have the surgery. I am looking forward to that appointment to hear what she will say. But we all are getting older. We need to pay attention to our bodies. I exercise and walk more because I'm not in such pain as I was before. I walk the track and do at least four laps.

There are three things that I am doing now. I exercise more. Mentally, I feel freer. I am making decisions to better myself. I did not allow the cost to hinder my decision. I share what I have learned with others. I am not active in organizations yet because I am still gathering information.

I want to thank God. I also want to thank my husband, and my dad. They were so very supportive of me and my journey. I also want to thank Dr. Lipman. He made me feel very comfortable with the procedure. My husband was with me during the procedure. My waist shrunk. I just feel healthier. I just want to get my story out and hopefully save a life. Getting this story out about fibroids is important. I also want to help others to know that there are options. We miss the clues about the changes in our bodies. We have to pay attention to our bodies. Having options are key to taking care of our bodies.

Teacher: Ms. Moreira, thank you so much for sharing your Powerful Health Decision with us.   Your story is also very powerful. I just know that your story as well as the stories of all of our speakers on their Powerful Health and Wellness Decisions will help someone who is going through their own challenges now.   Class, join me in thanking each of our speakers.

It is now homework time class:

1. Are you currently going through a health and wellness challenge?_____

_____

2. Did you learn anything from our speakers to help you take the next steps in your journey? _____

_____

_____

_____

_____

_____

3. Are you paying attention to your body? _____

_____

_____

4. Are you getting the necessary information that you need to

   deal with your challenge? _____

_____

_____

_____

5. Are you taking care of your body? _____

_____

_____

6. What can you do right now to make a better decision and

   take care of your body? _____

_____

_____

_____

_____

_____

_____

CHAPTER 5: POWERFUL DECISIONS IN THE CLASSROOM OF YOUR FINANCIAL LIFE

Teacher: Class, this next session is on finance.   What exactly is finance? To put it as simply as possible, it is all about money. Do you have any money? Do you have enough money? How do you earn your money? How do you want to earn your money? What do you know about making your money grow? Do you have any debt? Do you have any credit cards? Do you have any investments? What is your credit score? I know that these are a lot of questions. But money and finance are very important. We have a number of guest speakers who will share their Powerful Financial Decisions and how we can learn from them to help us make better decisions with our finances.

Our guest speaker is Ms. Theresa Barnabei.   Let's welcome her to our classroom. Please tell us a little about you Ms. Barnabei.

Powerful Decisions in the Classrooms of Life

Ms. Barnabei: I live in Tucson, Arizona and I have a bachelor's degree. I am an Intuitive Coach and an Inspirational Educator.

Teacher: Please share with us your Powerful Financial Decision.

Ms. Barnabei: When I was in grade school, I remember making a decision that I wanted to have enough money to do what I wanted, and when I wanted. Growing up very aware of this decision, I was always thinking forward and looking for business opportunities. As I grew up and got my first real job, I wasn't very smart about my money! When I launched my own business many years later, I knew I had to put a smart money system in place so I didn't repeat the same mistakes I made previously. My smart money system consisted of 4 buckets:

1. The 1st bucket was to hold 10% at a minimum of all revenues I brought in every month;

2. The 2nd bucket held 30% of everything I brought in to ensure I always had enough money to pay my taxes;

3. The 3rd was 15% of everything I made was earmarked to put back into my business; and

4. The remaining 45% was paid to my household to cover my living expenses.

Then I realized that if I didn't have a plan for the 45%, I would spend it just because I had it!   So, from there, I created more buckets:

   a. I allocated a small percentage of whatever was left over after paying my bills;

   b. I had a "save-to-spend" account, which was money I set aside so that I could do or buy whatever I wanted, as long as there was money in the account;

   c. Then there was my vacation fund so that if I wanted to go on a trip, all I needed to see is if I had the money in the account; and

      d.   An "emergency fund" account was available for those unforeseen expenses that popped up like car repairs, or appliance replacements.

When I funded all of my accounts, which was really easy once I set up a system to do so. I had financial freedom on a daily basis, being able to do what I wanted, if I wanted because the money was there!

Teacher: Wow, this is a very impressive money management system. What did you learn from setting up this system?

Ms. Barnabei: Having a goal and a plan to achieve it is what moves everything into a reality.

Teacher: How did your life change from this decision?

Ms. Barnabei: I am living the life of my dreams! I learned the system pretty much on my own, but my financial planner did help me refine it and for him, I am grateful. As you can tell by all the buckets I created, that every aspect of my life that is touched by money is impacted.

Teacher: Is there anything else about this decision that you would like to share with the class?

Ms. Barnabei: Anyone can change their current situation with focus and intention. With clarity around what you want, why you want it, plus the desire to achieve it, the "how" to make it happen will always show itself. All things will line up in perfect order, but you have to pay attention and take action. Then trust that it is coming to you!

Teacher: Thank you again Ms. Barnabei. You really have me thinking about my current money management plan.

Class, I want to end this chapter with some additional information on money and finance. First, make the Powerful Decision to win the game of Money! Money may be paper (bills), metal (coins), or plastic (credit cards), but it is always very important in life. We heard the term, "Money is the root of all evil." This is one of the misquoted passages of the Bible. The accurate quote is, "the Love of money is the root of all evil."(1 Timothy 6:10). Money, in and of itself, is neither good nor bad. The more money you have the more options you have to do things. Your money only magnifies the type of person that you are on the inside. If you have more money, you can help yourself and others or you can ignore helping yourself and others. You get to choose.

Let's examine one of the three necessities of life – food, clothing, and shelter. Shelter represents the type of place where you want to live and lay your head down to sleep and rest. It may be a house with a yard and white picket fence, an apartment, a condo, a townhouse, or a mansion. If it is a house with a white picket fence, what neighborhood do you want to live in? Is the house an asset or just a place to live? Beginning with the end in mind, there are some important things to consider before the purchase.

1. How long do you plan on living in the house? 3 years – 5 years– 7 years – 10 years, until the children graduate from high school or forever because this is the dream house?

2. If you are planning on living in the house for a short amount of time, what is the exit strategy before buying the house? Are you going to keep the house and rent it out or are you going to sell it when you move? The answers could dictate the location, size, and amenities of the house.

3. How many bedrooms should this house have?

4. What is the status of the school district where the house will be located?

5. What is the crime rate in the area where you are thinking about buying your house?

6. What has been the rate of property value growth over the last 3 – 5 years?

These are but a few of the pertinent questions you must answer so that this financial decision will be a powerful one. Price cannot be the only factor that you look at when making a purchase. A deal in price is not a deal if the house is in the wrong neighborhood, is located in a poor school district, or the property value in the area is declining. Who will be the buyer for your property when you are ready to move on if these questions are not taken into consideration before the purchase?

Even if you have the right property in the right area, how will you finance the house? Will it be a traditional 30-year fixed mortgage, a 15-year fixed mortgage, an interest-only mortgage, an Adjustable Rate Mortgage (ARM), or other types of mortgage? Do you fully understand each of these types of mortgages and which financial decision each one makes the most sense to utilize in your purchase? You need the information, without emotion, to make a powerful decision. Don't let ignorance prevent you from making the right choice. Most mortgage payments, other than the interest-only mortgage, are made up of interest and principal repayment.

Example: House for $200,000. The interest rate is 4%. With a traditional 30-year fixed rate mortgage, the payment is $954.83 per month. Over the 30-year life of the loan, you pay back to the lender, not $200,000; but $343,738.80. Bank made $143,738.80 in interest. On the first payment, you made to the lender of $954.83 only $288.16 went to repay the principal and $666.67 went to the interest! After 5 years, the mortgage picture looks like this: The balance on the loan is $180,895.15. The principal paid is $19,105.85. The interest paid is $38,184.95. The total payments made are $57,289.80. You can get an amortization schedule from your lender that breaks down the payment distribution over the life of the loan. There is so much more information on purchasing a home. Get educated before you make your purchase and know your why and your exit strategy before you buy. Buying a house by:

- Getting a traditional mortgage without considering all of your options;

- Never refinancing (on purpose);

- Doubling up on payments and putting extra towards the principal;

- Paying off the house early;

- Burning the mortgage; **but**

- Having no money saved for retirement;

- Having no college funds for your children; **and**

- Having no money for travel and fun, etc., is **not** exercising your power in the financial classroom.

Now, you find yourself in your golden years, we are going through the biggest recession since the great depression, and some things have happened beyond your control. The eqity you were sitting on in your home has been severely diminished. Some of your neighbors may have lost a job and have had their homes foreclosed on. This event, even though it did not happen to you, you were impacted. The neighborhood property values declined and a substantial amount of your equity is now gone. You are older and you may have health challenges where additional financial funds are needed to cover these expenses. You may just need additional financial resources because of inflation. Everything just costs more. Since you are on a fixed income, you are looking at all of your options for funds. You may have to consider tapping into the equity in your paid-off house. You may not be able to qualify for a traditional mortgage or even a line of credit on the equity of your home because of no employment, credit rating, and other things that the lender considers for your ability to repay the mortgage. So, here you are with a house with equity locked into the walls of the home and no way to get it out and liquidity the equity to meet your financial means.

Another powerful question to ask yourself in this finance classroom is "Do you want to be rich or do you want to be debt-free first?" Before making any financial decisions, consider what you would like your financial life to look like. You may have heard the term, "Pay yourself first." What does that mean? What about keeping a ready reserve of cash before you shift to paying off cars, homes, credit cards, etc? Everyone needs an emergency fund. If you do not have an emergency fund, then everything that happens to you becomes an emergency. How much should one have put away for an emergency? First, how much is one month of your expenses: your tithes and offerings at church, gifts to charities, food, insurance, incidentals, mortgage/rent, utilities, transportation, internet, cable, phone, etc? This total amount equals your debt-freedom number. Based on what you have in savings now and you lost your current source of income, how many days/months/years of freedom do you have? Do you have 1 day, 3 months, 6 months, 1 year, or 0 days of freedom? This financial freedom amount is called "Peace of Mind." Based on the most recent recession which has been described as the worst recession since the Great Depression of the 1920s, 6 months to 1 year minimum should be the amount of an emergency fund that you should strive to maintain. So again, if you lost your job and source of income, how many months could you maintain your current standard of living and pay all your bills without panicking? Obviously, 1 month is not enough for an emergency fund. Make another Powerful Financial Decision to go for at least a 6-month to 1-year worth of an emergency fund. After this fund is in place in an account that is separate from your regular checking account, then you can consider attacking other financial decisions, including maybe paying off debts. The emergency fund is probably one of your most important financial decisions.

Another Powerful Financial Decision to make is how to apportion your finances in general. Do you know where your finances are going? What percentage is going toward debts, living, charity and church giving, fun, waste, etc.? Consider making a financial statement, personal balance sheet, and a BUDGET. Treat your finances like a successful business. You have to know your numbers. What is the total income coming into the household, total expenses going out of the household, and how much is left over, or is a definite amount needed to cover your monthly expenses? Some people operate on a deficiency in their monthly expenses. There is more month at the end of their money. They shoot from the hip and don't know where their money goes. They use or misuse credit cards to get them to the next payday for the household. To move from deficient to excess, you have to either increase the income of funds into the household or reduce the amount of money incurred on expenses. But making these financial documents initially shows you where you are starting from. This knowledge is powerful. You make not like your current reality, but remember to Begin with the End in Mind.

How would you like your financial life to look? Some financial experts suggest a plan of 10-10-80 as a viable financial plan. Some suggest a 10-10-10-70 plan. There are other plans for you to consider, but let's look at these two plans. 10-10-80 is where you allocate 10% of your total income to God, and 10% of your total income is allocated to your savings, emergency funds, and/or long-term financial goals. The last 80% of your total income is allocated to your living expenses of food, clothing, shelter, insurance, etc. The 10-10-10-70 plan is similar to the previous plan, except that another 10% of the total income is allocated to fun things. Just like a diet, people sometimes cheat and eat and do things that are not on their diet plan. Sometimes, having an off day or free day to do those things and eat those things helps you to stay on the plan for the other six days. So, this extra 10% that you use for play helps you to enjoy living now and not after being so financially strict in saving all the time without enjoying life. Use this account for shopping, movies, fun activities, going to the spa, out to eat for fun, and any other recreational activities you enjoy doing. There are other financial plans for you to consider, but do yourself a favor and make your own plan. Now, with a plan for how you want your financial life to look, your future will be better. But also know that making a plan is only the first step. Now, follow your plan immediately. You will review and make adjustments to your plan as you continue living. Things change and having a grip on your financial life will be key to being able to adapt to those changes.

Let's discuss some of the options for savings and investments. These terms do not mean the same thing. Savings, money put aside for future use, can be saved in a shoe box, a paper bag, bank or credit union savings account. Money placed in the first two options – shoe box and paper bag - earns zero interest. Your savings could be subject to total loss due to theft or fire to the hiding place of your savings. Savings in the bank or credit union provides a safer place to save your money. The bank or credit union pays you interest. However, the amount of interest you receive for maintaining a savings account is very little.

Compound interest is when your interest earns interest. "Remember that money is of a prolific generating nature. Money can beget money, and its offspring can beget more." Benjamin Franklin and Albert Einstein said, "Compounding is mankind's greatest invention because it allows for the reliable, systematic accumulation of wealth." Compound interest has been called the "Eighth Wonder of the World." Those who understand it will earn it and those who don't will pay for it. We can't discuss interest or compound interest without reviewing the **Rule of 72**. This rule is one of the most important money rules. When you put away money in any type of financial vehicle – savings account, CD, money market, mutual funds, stocks, etc., you want your money to grow and even double. So knowing the Rule of 72 allows you to know how long it takes for your money to double. Apply the Rule of 72: Divide 72 by the annual interest rate of return you are getting on your investment. The result is the number of years it will take to double your money! Example: you open a savings account with $500.00 in a bank. The bank is paying 5% interest (annual percentage rate). 72 divided by 5 = 14.4. This means that your $500.00 in the savings account will double to $1,000 in 14 years and 4 months without any other deposits into this account and the 5% did not change throughout the entire 14.40 years. Can you wait for 14.4 years for your money to double? However, if the current stated best interest rate for savings accounts is less than 1%, applying the Rule of 72 to the current numbers would be worse. 72 divided by 1 = 72 years! This rule and current results should encourage you to review and examine other options for your money. There is no one size fits all for your Powerful Financial Decisions. You may have many accounts for the many goals you are pursuing. Each investment option has various components of safety, amount of interest paid, accessibility of your funds via checks or debit cards, time to receive funds when needed, the performance of the investment, experience of the individuals and/or company that is making the investment decisions of your funds, and many other components.

Consider this example: One of the greatest basketball players ever is Michael Jordan. Even though Michael is retired, he continues to enjoy a lucrative income from the Air Jordan tennis shoes by Nike. The average cost of the shoe is $130.00. A share of Nike stock on August 13, 2013 is about $66.00. How many people who own a pair of Air Jordan tennis shoes also own at least 1 share of Nike stock? Are you just a consumer of the product or do you own a share/piece/percentage of the company that makes the product? Look around your house and in your closets and see what products you purchase. Tide or Gain washing powder, Crest or Aim toothpaste, Dove or Ivory soap, Mayfield or Ben & Jerry's ice cream, Nike or Adidas tennis shoes, Levi or Wrangler jeans, Polo or Calvin Klein cologne, Dooney & Burke or Michael Kors handbags? We buy a lot of stuff and some of us are loyal to specific brands. If you like the stuff/product, have you ever considered buying stock in the companies that produce the stuff you like? You can do some basic research on the companies via the internet by going to the company's websites. But again "Begin with the End in Mind" knowing why you are investing. Investing of any type has a measure of risk. There are no guarantees of any type with any investment option. As stated earlier, saving money in a shoe box or a paper bag is risky too due to fire and/or theft.

Buying stock in a company gives you a percentage of ownership in that company. Prices of stock go up and come down. No one has a crystal ball to predict what will happen. But the basic premise of buying stock is to "buy when the price is low and sell when the stock is high" to produce a profit (the difference in the prices) for you. You may also have heard the saying, "Don't put all of your eggs in a single basket." Since you don't know what will happen in the future, you could guess wrong and your eggs will all break like Humpty Dumpty. However, another financial expert, Robert Kiyosaki, states, "Put all of your eggs in a single basket, but watch that basket." Meaning knowing and researching the right basket and keeping watch over its performance as you anticipated it to perform. But again, be careful. Consult the financial experts before you make your moves.

Another financial move to make is to invest using a mutual fund. You are not just buying a share of only one company, but you are buying a share percentage of many different companies which spreads the risk of investing in the wrong company at the wrong time. www.morningstar.com is a good website to get information about many types of investment vehicles, including mutual funds. Morningstar has even done some research on many factors of investing and provided a simple tool, its star ranking guide, to assist you in your decisions. Some people are very conservative in their approach to investing, and some are riskier in their approach. Morningstar assigned its highest star rating of 5 stars (*****) to those investment options so that you can make a Powerful Financial Decision on investing. Morningstar examines the past performance of the investment vehicle, the managers' experience, performance compared to others inside its sector, etc. A lot of this information is available for free. You can get information on how much it costs to open an account with a particular mutual fund, if it is even open to new investors, the fees charged by the fund, if any, and other valuable information. Remember, past performance does not guarantee the future performance of any type of investment; it is just one item to consider.

Class, I hope that you also are thinking about your current money management plan as well.

It is homework time class:

1. Do you currently have a money management plan? _____

   _____

2. If not, will you make the decision to develop your plan?

   _____

3. If you do have a plan, what categories/buckets are a part of

   your plan? _____

   _____

   _____

   _____

   _____

   _____

   _____

   _____

4. How clear are you on your goals for your money

    management plan? _____

    _____

    _____

    _____

    _____

    _____

    _____

    _____

CHAPTER 6: POWERFUL DECISIONS IN THE CLASSROOM OF YOUR ESTATE PLANNING LIFE

Teacher: Class, we are almost at the end of our classrooms

and examination of the Powerful Decisions that we have made in

each of the classrooms. Now, let's discuss your Estate Plan. You

have spent almost your entire life obtaining stuff. What happens

to your stuff when you are no longer alive? This area can disrupt

lives for generations. Do you have a will, advance directives, or even life insurance? You have worked hard all of your life, you have a house, a car, money in the bank, furniture, clothes, dishes, quilts, jewelry, and a pet. Who gets your things when you die? Sometimes, people would rather forget this part of their lives in hopes that they can escape this life without dying. However, we all will die one day. Dying without a last will can lead to consequences that you may not intend nor even know how your state will make a decision of who gets your stuff. Do you know people, friends, and family members, who died without a last will and/or without life insurance? Everyone knows someone who died without insurance to cover the burial and the family members had to contribute to the funeral expenses. Sometimes, the funeral had to be delayed until the funds were collected to pay for the burial.

Let's begin with life insurance. Who needs life insurance? How much insurance? What type of life insurance do you need to get? Do you need to get life insurance for your children? In the simplest definition, life insurance is a contract between the policyholder and the life insurance company that provides for payment of a sum of money to a named beneficiary upon the death of the policyholder when he/she dies. Example: You buy a life insurance policy with a face amount of $100,000.00. When you die, the beneficiaries (whom you select), will receive a check from the insurance company for $100,000.00. Does everyone need life insurance? No. If you are wealthy and have the funds in your investment accounts for your final expenses and to leave money to your heirs/beneficiaries, then you may not need a life insurance policy. However, most people are not in a place financially where they do not need life insurance. So, how much should you get? Let's use another definition for life insurance. When you are young, after graduating from high school, you are beginning your adult life. You may continue your education in college or a technical school, you begin to work, you buy stuff, you get married, you have children, and you begin your adult life. Especially when you start to acquire things, like a house and car, those things are usually financed with a mortgage and a car loan. You have things and you have debt. Your income and your spouse's income finance your life. If your income is being used to pay for your expenses, then you need to look at enough life insurance to cover your income in the event you died while you are in the acquiring/high-earning period of your life.

Example: Husband earns $75,000.00 per year and wife earns $55,000.00 per year. They have two children, 12 years old and 10 years old. They have a house, two cars, three credit cards, and other expenses. The husband is 35 years old and the wife is 33 years old. Usually, it takes both incomes to meet the monthly expenses of the family. So, both husband and wife need life insurance. If either of them died, then the surviving spouse would surely miss the income that the deceased spouse earned during his/her lifetime. A simple formula for the amount of insurance that each spouse needs is 10 X the yearly income earned. So, using this formula, the husband needs at least a $750,000.00 life insurance policy and the wife needs at least a $550,000.00 life insurance policy. I am sure that you are asking why this amount. Suppose the husband dies an untimely death. The wife would receive a check from the insurance company for $750,000.00. That is a lot of money, and money without instructions will soon disappear. The money is not for her to go on a no-holds-barred shopping spree and buy new cars, new furniture, new clothes, trips, toys, gifts to family (disguised as loans), etc. She should immediately put the money in an annuity or investment that pays her a monthly income of about 10% which equals what the husband was earning while he was alive. His income has been replaced and the lifestyle of the family can remain intact. She is living off the interest earned from the insurance proceeds and the principal amount, $750,000.00 is still there. If she spends the principal, then the interest that could have been earned is lost forever. She can always spend the principal later, like when the children graduate from college, or never leave the principal for her children or even her children's children. This plan obviously makes sense logically for the family to do. But the next question is what type of life insurance should the family buy?

There are basically two types of life insurance – Whole life and term. Whole life is a policy that provides permanent insurance with an investment fund. The payments that you pay, usually on a monthly basis, are split between the two – part of your premium goes to the insurance, and part of your premium goes to the investment and builds cash value that you can borrow against without being taxed by Uncle Sam. There are two major subtypes of whole life insurance – Universal Life and Variable Life. Universal life combines the term life insurance with a money market-type of investment. The rate of return on the investment [ROI] is usually not guaranteed. Variable life combines the term life insurance with an investment fund tied to the stock or bond mutual fund investment. Again, the rate of return on the investment is not guaranteed. The amount of the premium usually does not change during the life of the policy, your whole life. However, the amount can be rather an expensive financial obligation to the policyholder.

The other major type of life insurance is a term insurance policy. There is no investment part of this type of policy. But it is for a specific time period of 10 years, 15 years, 20 years, or even 30 years. The premium for this type of insurance is very affordable and much lower than the whole-life type of insurance. At the end of the stated term, the policy either ends or renews at a higher premium amount.

There is also a remaining question on the topic of life insurance – do children need life insurance? Based on the realistic definition we are using regarding income contributions to the family, then unless your child (ren) is/are producing income for the family to live on, then there may not be a need for life insurance on a child. Is your child an entertainer, professional athlete, or business owner producing a profit, or just a regular child that is not producing income? If not, then there may not be a need for life insurance; but only if the family has the investment funds with a balance sufficient to pay for the final funeral/burial expenses due to the untimely death of a child.

Powerful Decisions in the Classrooms of Life

Now that the parties have their insurance needs met, let's talk about advance directives. What is an advance directive? Why do you need one? An advance directive is a legal document that is the combination of several other legal documents – a living will, health care, power of attorney, and a directive to physicians. When a person is unable to communicate or is mentally incapable of communicating with his/her physicians regarding the utilization of medical procedures and/or treatment to be kept alive or not to be kept alive. The importance of having an advanced directive was brought to life with the case of Theresa Marie Schindler (Terri) Schiavo. Terri married Michael Schiavo in 1986. In 1990, at the age of 26, Terri suffered a mysterious cardio-respiratory arrest for which no cause has ever been determined. She was diagnosed with hypoxic encephalopathy - a neurological injury caused by a lack of oxygen to the brain. Terri was placed on a ventilator, but was soon able to breathe on her own and maintain vital function. She remained in a severely compromised neurological state and was provided a PEG tube to ensure the safe delivery of nourishment and hydration. On

March 31, 2005, Terri Schindler Schiavo died of marked dehydration following more than 13 days without nutrition or hydration under the order of Circuit Court Judge, George W. Greer of the Pinellas-Pasco's Sixth Judicial Court. Terri was 41. This case was a situation where Terri did not have an advanced directive that she has executed to let her desire know about the medical treatment she would like. Her husband and her parents were each trying to make decisions for her because she could not. There were many court actions that the husband eventually won. He stated that Terri would not want to be kept alive in the current medical state that she was in. Her parents wanted her to be kept alive.

Everyone needs to clearly state their intentions on this matter. In an advanced directive, you define what you want your intentions to be in the case that you are in a terminal condition and what type of medical decisions to be made. You can appoint a person to act on your behalf with the physicians in making the appropriate decisions. Don't leave this part of your life to chance or create life-long feelings of betrayal among family members. You may also want your doctor to have a copy of your advance directives. Most hospitals will ask if you have one if you are admitted for a medical procedure. You may also want your agent or your designee that you name to have a copy so he/she will know what to do.

The last topic in this classroom for this class is a **Last Will and Testament (hereinafter referred to as Will)**. A Will is a declaration of whom you would like to have the things you have accumulated while you are living when you die. The lack of a Will can create some consequences that you may not have intended. Be clear on what your State laws are regarding your Will. Do not assume that you know what your state law requires.

Example: In the state of Georgia, if a person dies without a will, then state law determines who are the heirs (recipients) of your belongings. Suppose there are a husband, a wife, and two children. The husband dies without a will. The husband's belongings are equally owned by the wife and the two children;

not by the wife only. If there are more children, then the spouse is guaranteed at least a 1/3 interest in the things of the husband. If one of the children dies before the parent, then their children (grandchildren) would receive their parent's share.

Having a Will is not a one-time event. You should review your documents to make sure that you do not need to make any changes to those documents. As it relates to a Will, some events will automatically void a Will – a divorce, having more children, etc. Again, know what the laws in your state requires on this issue. So, review your documents to make sure that they are current to your wishes and desires. You also want to think about where to keep these documents. A safe deposit box, your lawyer's office, the probate court's office, or a fireproof home safe are places to consider. Again, you are beginning with the end in mind to make powerful decisions and take powerful actions to handle your estate.

Homework:

1. What is your current grade in the class of Estate Planning?

    _____

    _____

2. Do you have life insurance? _____

    _____

3. Do you have an Advance Directive? _____

    _____

4. Do you have a Last Will and Testament? _____

    _____

5. Do you need additional help in this area? _____

    _____

CHAPTER 7: POWERFUL DECISIONS
SUMMARY

Teacher: When you look at your life as a classroom, you

realize that there are many classes that you must take.   First,

learn the lesson, then take the test, and then pass the test. If you do not pass the test, there will be a re-testing. Everyone alive is in various classes and at different levels in each of their classes. There is one thing that you must know - you will always be in a class until you take your last breath. While you are still breathing, there is a lesson that you must learn and/or teach someone else. You will keep growing by learning the lessons until you pass the test or you will be repeating a lesson and test over and over again. Once you know how you want your ending to be, you can get started with gathering the information, learning from others, and making your success plan for a powerful outcome for your life.

The graduates that you have met throughout this book have shared their powerful decisions with you because they wanted to give back to those coming behind them in that particular class. Learn from their powerful decisions to help you with making your own powerful decisions.

<u>Next steps:</u>

1. Do you know where you are in each of the life

    classrooms? _____

    _____

    _____

    _____

    _____

    _____

    _____

    _____

2. How powerful have your decisions been so far? _____

    _____

    _____

    _____

_____ -

_____

_____

3. Did you have a plan for success where you began with

    the end in mind first? _____

    _____

    _____

    _____

    _____

    _____

4. Do you want to pass the test that you may have been

    repeating over and over again? _____

    _____

    _____

    _____

    _____

5. Are you stuck in a class? _____

_____

_____

_____

_____

_____

6. Do you need a mentor or coach in an area where you

   are stuck? _____

_____

_____

_____

_____

_____

Teacher: Class, you should really take a look at your life

and do something. Many of you may have heard the definition

of insanity – doing the same thing over and over again, but

expecting a different result. If you keep doing the same thing, you will keep getting the same results. In order for things to change, you must change. I wish for everyone in class to make a Powerful Decision and have a Wonderful Life. Class has ended for today. Don't forget about your homework.

Message from the Author:

Do you have a Powerful Decision that you would like to share in the next edition of *"Powerful Decisions in the Classrooms of Life"* book? Please contact the author at Sharon@Powerof1Decision.com for more information.

Made in the USA
Columbia, SC
19 January 2023

75622993R00109